How Much Should I Charge?

How Much Should I Charge?

Pricing Basics for Making Money Doing What You Love

ELLEN ROHR

MAXROHR

ROGERSVILLE, MISSOURI

For information about this text or the material within, contact the publisher at:
Phone: 1-877-MAXROHR
E-mail: ellen@maxrohr.com
         www.maxrohr.com

Publisher's Cataloging-in-Publication Data
Rohr, Ellen.
     How much should I charge?: pricing basics for making money doing what you
     love / Ellen Rohr. — Rogersville, MO: MAXROHR Press, 1999.
          p.   ill.   cm.
          ISBN 0-9665719-1-6
     1. Pricing. 2. Small business—finance. I. Title.
HF5416.5 .R64   1999   99-60691
658.8'16   dc—21   CIP

PROJECT COORDINATION BY JENKINS GROUP, INC.

03 02 01 00 ◆ 5 4 3 2 1

Printed in the United States of America

To Max Rohr.

Corporate vice president, savvy marketer, astute investor, talented artisan,

wonderful person and perfect son.

Thanks for choosing us.

Love, Mom

Contents

Acknowledgments

Lots of folks influenced the creation of this helpful book! Thanks to Hot Rod, Max, Dan, Al, Frank, Matt, Lance, Lynn, Tae, Gail, Jim, Eleanor, Nic, John, James, Eric, Ambur, Becky, Chin, Pat, Rachel, Kelly, Brenda, Steve, Kay, Rhonda, Melina, Manola, Harry, Julie, Cindy, Charlotte, Mel C., Madonna, Jack, Lauryn, Amanda, Susie, Nikki, Eric, Jerry, Theresa, Luke, Misha, Mary Jo, Mark Victor, Laurie, Bob, Sally, Joey, Mrs. Fernwicky, Mike, Lyle, Ken, Pepper, Rocket, Hazel, Felix, Garfield, Cher, and Oprah.

I couldn't have done it without you!

xoxoxo — Ellen

Some tips for using this book...

1. Have your own financial statements handy. A current balance sheet and income statement is good. If you have last year's statements, pull them out as well. When I present financial information and terms, see if you can find that info in your reports. I want you to use this material to help make your dreams come true! *It's only worth knowing if it's worth **using**.*

2. If you aren't comfortable with reading these reports refer to *Where Did the Money Go?* — the first book in the Business Basics series. It defines all the terms and teaches you what the financial statements *are* and why on earth you would want to read them! "How Much...?" is the second book in this bare-bones-basics series.

3. This is a beginner's book. You will graduate from this material and reach for other great business books and resources as your knowledge and awareness develops. But this book series assumes you know nothing about business. So if you want to start at the beginning, you've come to the right place.

4. The examples in this book work best for a company that sells *time.* Do you sell your expertise? Do you sell your labor? If you are a contractor, hair cutter, consultant, landscaper, accountant, artist, lawyer, doctor, baby-sitter, massage therapist, designer, bookkeeper, house cleaner, systems analyst...**this book was written expressly for you.**

5. If you sell products, terrific! This book will be useful. Time is still the most precious commodity. How many hours a day do you have to sell your products? You can always create more products. You only have so much *time.*

6. Be willing to suspend your current beliefs about business. The standard rules for business are WRONG. If most businesses fail — and about 80% are out of business or losing money within the first few years of operation — why would you want to follow commonly accepted business practices? I suggest that most of the financial advice available to small businesses is based on bad information!! So there.

7. You must keep score, with hard numbers. This book isn't about affirmations and divine intervention, though I believe in those things as strongly as the concepts I present in this book. It's not enough to believe, you must act. *Trust in God, but tie your camel.*

8. Don't expect to become an expert overnight. Learning how to use numbers to make better management decisions is a process.

9. You will make fewer management mistakes — I promise — when you use numbers to guide you. Learning to use your costs to plan for the future, set goals, set selling prices and get where you want to go with your business...**that's what this book will do for you.**

10. You can always call me for help! My toll-free number is 877.MAXROHR (877.629.7347) Let me know if there is something you don't understand. I will do my best to clear things up!

10 GREAT REASONS TO READ AND UNDERSTAND
How Much Should I Charge?

1. You want to make money in your business.

2. You've been basing your selling prices on what the other guy charges — and you just found out that the other guy is going out of business.

3. You've discovered the 'going rate' is good for one thing...going down the drain.

4. You have plenty of hobbies. You don't want your business to be another one.

5. You have been pulling selling prices out of thin air and you don't want to do that anymore!

6. You read all the business *For Dummies...* books, and now you feel like a real dummy. The information was too complicated! You want **easy.** This is it.

7. You want to do what you love, and you want to make a decent living doing it.

8. You have been in business for years...and you have less money than before you started.

9. You are thinking about starting a business and you are wise enough to look into pricing *before* you lose lots of money.

10. You want to **make LOTS of money** in your business.

Why I wrote this book...

"How did you come up with your selling price?" Frank asked me.

"Well, uh, we base our prices on what the market will bear," I stammered.

"Quit saying 'we'. I know you are the one who sets the prices at your company," he pressed. "How did you come up with your price?"

I started to sweat. "Based on the going rate for plumbing services in our area, we, er, I, charge $30 per hour."

He kept after me, "Do all the other plumbers charge $30 per hour?"

"No, some charge as much as $45 an hour. But I think that's ripping people off," I answered righteously.

"Oh, really. Well, how much is it costing you to be in business? What is your break-even cost per hour?"

I wondered what he was talking about! I went to business school. I knew that the marketplace determined how much you could charge. There was a limit on what folks would pay. They didn't care how much it cost you to provide the service. It was your job to figure out how to make money at the going rate selling price. Right??

Frank Blau is a super successful plumbing contractor who took me under his wing. My husband, Hot Rod, and I ran a small plumbing company. And, we were starving. I had called Frank, whining about how little money we were making. What Frank said next dropped me in my tracks. "You are basing your selling price on what the other guys charge. What makes you think that they know what they are doing?"

"They seem so successful," I said. "I was at an association meeting the other night. I kept asking people, 'How's business?' and each one said, 'Business is great! We're really busy.'"

Frank chuckled, "Busy is easy. Profitability is more difficult. And there is only one way to be profitable. Charge more for your services than it costs to create them."

Well, *duh*! I got a little defensive. "Well, sure Frank, I mean. Isn't that obvious?"

He asked again, "How much is it costing you to be in business? What's your break-even point?"

I had no idea. **And I bet you don't either.**

That's why I wrote this book.

In my first book, *Where Did the Money Go?* you learned how to read financial statements. Good for you! That's essential. You must learn what a balance sheet is, what an income statement is. If you haven't read *Where Did the Money Go?*, stop right here and go back and read it. If you need a copy call me - toll-free - at 877.MAXROHR (877. 629.7647). Or check out www.maxrohr.com.

How Much Should I Charge? will help you learn more bare bones basic information about running your company. I'll keep it simple, and define all the fancy accounting and business terms as we go along. You'll learn how to use your financial information to create a selling price that will **make your dreams come true**.

Wouldn't that be nice?

Should? Could? Would? Will? Do!

I called this book *How Much Should I Charge?* because I hear that question, worded just that way, every single day.

"If the going rate won't cut it, how much should I charge?"

Let me explain that I don't like the word *should*. *Should* implies that you are doing something wrong now, and that you may or may not change your behavior. Should is a guilt-ridden word. New Age guru Louise Hay recommends crossing the word *should* right out of your vocabulary.

Instead ask, "How much *could* I charge?"

Hmmmm. This question has a different feel. Now, you are in charge. What are your options? How much *could* you charge?

Add up the dollars, figure out how much you need and want. At this point you might get excited about the prospect of actually making as much money as you want! You'll say, "How much would I charge if I decided to make my dreams come true?" With some encouragement, you'll progress to, "How much will I charge?" as your ability to take responsibility for your own well-being increases.

Ultimately, as you go through the information in this book, you'll learn to create a selling price based on *your* numbers, on *your* hopes and dreams and goals. Then you will be able to state with certainty and confidence...

"HOW MUCH *DO* I CHARGE? THIS MUCH_____!"

Don't be afraid of pricing yourself out of the market. Remember...

IT'S NOT 'WHAT THE MARKET WILL BEAR'... IT'S 'CAN YOU BEAR THE MARKET??'

If you took Economics 101 in high school or college, you learned that selling prices for goods and services are determined by what the market will bear. That means that consumers — the market — decide what a product or service is worth, and will give so much money, but no more, for that product or service.

After doing a fake-voice phone survey of a few companies, and setting your prices somewhere in their range, you might say you are charging what the market will bear. This beats going to the trouble of figuring out what your company's break-even point is. "We can't charge more than what the market will bear!" is delivered as a logical reason for maintaining below-cost selling prices.

But here's the rub. The what the market will bear rule only applies to commodities. Commodities are products that don't differ much from vendor to vendor. Gold, for instance, is a commodity. Gold is gold is gold. Gold will follow the economic rule of what the market will bear pretty nicely. It will be directly affected by the law of supply and demand. Economics 101 works well when you are talking about commodities.

But it doesn't count for much as far as *your* products and services go.

Here's the **real** rule, the 'street' rule, the rule they don't teach you in Economics 101: the market doesn't set the selling price. The *marketers* do.

  ▲ Why does Coca Cola sell for three times the price of Best Choice cola?

  ▲ How come Rolex sells watches for $50,000 when you can get a very nice watch for $100?

  ▲ Why would anyone pay $15,000 to cross the Atlantic on the Concord when a jet plane will get you there for about $500?

The marketers in this world differentiate their products, and make them something more than a commodity. Marketers create and communicate features that benefit consumers. Benefits add value to the product. Coke is the *real* thing. A Rolex is a symbol of wealth and power. And the Concord goes really fast. (*Speed* is always a cool product feature).

Higher value commands a higher price. But, there will be no sale unless value *exceeds* price. I heard a terrific explanation of this phenomenon by Harry J. Friedman. Harry says, "If value equals price, then there is no sale."

$$Value = Price = No\ Sale$$

Cash in pocket will only be exchanged for something that has a higher perceived value. So, if a product is worth exactly what you are charging for it, no one will buy it. What usually happens is that you will drop your price until the value of your product becomes bigger than the price.

$$Value > price;\ then,\ Sale$$

However, the marketer increases the value until the price looks insignificant.

$$VALUE > Price;\ then,\ profitable\ Sale$$

You see, there is a huge problem with basing your prices on what your competition is charging, on what the market will bear. I bet your competition is even more uneducated than you are when it comes to knowing his break-even and his true cost of doing business. He got his selling price by calling other companies, companies that are now out of business. Don't assume that your competitor knows what he is doing!

Lots of folks get confused when they set their selling prices. They look at what everyone else is charging, then they hope and pray that they can make money at those prices. So, don't beat yourself up.

When you confront how much your business really costs per year, per day, per hour, then you can set a realistic selling price. When you figure out what that selling price needs to be, it might scare you. Suppose your selling price is three times the going rate. It might be.

Can you *bear the market?* Yes. If you become a marketer. Set a real price, based on your costs. Then, establish why you're better and communicate that to your customers. It's possible. In fact, it's essential if you are going to get out of the 'commodities' rat race...and really make your dreams come true.

Is it easy? For some. Difficult for those who don't think they are worth very much. But why not try the formulas in this book? Assume that the world would be delighted to have the best of what you can uniquely offer with your services! And gladly pay for it.

Remember...

> *"Until YOU change, nothing will change for you."*
> JIM ROHN

OK, come clean...

How did you come up with the selling price that you are charging right now?

Write it down...

_____

_____

_____

_____

Did you...

▲ Call your competitor, assume a fake accent, and ask "How much do you charge for......." And then price your services within a few dollars of the answer??

▲ Pull a number out of thin air....close your eyes and pick a number?

▲ Avoid the issue altogether...every job is different so you just wing it, depending on what you think the customer can afford.

It's all right. Everyone makes these mistakes. I just want you to confront what you have been doing. The really smart folks, you for instance, recognize that these are ridiculous ways to set a selling price! And commit to learn a more reasonable method. That's what you'll learn in the upcoming pages.

Introducing...Sally Johnson!!

Every story needs a hero...or heroine. Introducing Sally Johnson. You are going to like Sally. And I bet you find that you and Sally have a lot in common.

Sally is 40 years old, married, with two kids...Suzy, who is 12 years old, and Mike, who's 8. Until very recently, she worked as a receptionist for a car dealer. It was a fun job. She loved her co-workers. And, her boss was really flexible with her schedule, which was important when her kids were little. But since Mike entered first grade, Sally has worked full time.

The car dealership gig was just a job to Sally. Her real passion was her house, her home. Sally is incredibly creative! She loves to paint....all over the walls! Every room in her house is a work of art. A mural of Narnia and *The Lion, The Witch and The Wardrobe* adorns Suzy's room. Mike has a NASCAR track in full action winding around all four walls in his room. In the rest of the house, Suzy has layered the walls with dramatic shades of tan and peach.

Sally taught herself the art of 'faux finishing'. It's a special painting technique. You apply the paint to the walls, and smudge it off with a rag or a sponge. Sounds easy, but it will look *awful*...unless you know what you are doing! Sally perfected her technique by practicing, over and over, on the walls of her home. She also creates wonderful murals: beautiful, wall-sized paintings of storybook characters, sports figures...whatever! Sally's husband, Bill, is a patient fellow. He has moved the furniture and painting equipment from here to there about a hundred times over the last 10 years, as Sally developed her skills.

Sally's husband's name is Bill but everyone calls him "Big Dog", which was his stage name when he toured with WCWI — World Class Wrestling, Inc. — as a tag-team champion. Big Dog is really a pussycat. Loves his family and lives a good life. He has a good job as a mail carrier. Unfortunately, most of Big Dog's paycheck goes to support the four kids he has by his first three wives. As a result, Sally is the primary breadwinner in the Johnson household.

It was Big Dog who convinced Sally to quit her job at the car dealership, and that is how Sally came to be the heroine of this book! "Sally, you should go into business for yourself," he urged. "You are so talented! You could make a ton of money painting other people's houses."

Sally had been thinking the same thing. She was ready for a change. She was 40 years old...it was now or never! So that's how Sally decided to go into business for herself. Let's tag along and see how well she does....

In this book, we'll follow Sally as she figures out how much she should charge for her wonderful services. In the process you'll discover some new ways of looking at selling prices and a formula for developing a selling price for your services. I hope that this information is helpful to you.

But, I need to make something very clear: if your life is working for you, if you have all that you ever dreamed of and more money than you can spend...then, **ignore everything in this book.**

However...if you aren't making any money in your business, well what have you got to lose? I wrote this book for you. You might want to try out these formulas. Go for it.

Remember that you are responsible for your life and your business. You are in charge of your own happiness. I can't guarantee that your business will succeed. But I know, as sure as I know I need one more breath to survive, that if you use numbers and dollars to track your progress in business, if you keep score...you can't be beat.

You can choose to stay in business or fold, whatever suits you best. Your call. You are not simply at the effect of a runaway company. Use the numbers to keep track, to keep score, to see how you are doing.

Would you like to make more money? Would you like to make a living doing what you love? It is absolutely 100% possible! And using Sally's company as an example, I am going to help you learn how to do it.

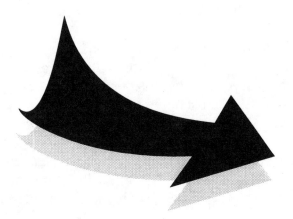

How much should you charge??

Before we begin, take this quiz!

1. I'm doing just what I want to do. I love my work! I am of service to others. I make as much money as I want. My family is taken care of financially. My retirement funds are more than adequate should I live to be 100 years old. My employees have careers, not just jobs, and they are building their investments with a company-funded retirement plan.

    True or False?

If you answered 'True', put this book down. You don't need it.

If you answered 'False', you are in the right place. Read on!!

Lunch with Joey

Sally and Joey Paterno have been friends since high school. He never asked her out, and she wouldn't have gone if he had. She always thought he was kind of a nerd. But they have always been good buddies.

Now, Joey owns a computer repair company called "The Revenge of the Geeks." He's done very well with his business. He has all the trappings of wealth: cool car, big house, Italian shoes. Yet, Joey is very down-to-earth. He puts together the St. Patrick's Day parade every year and sponsors the Senior Center activity programs. This fall the group is going to Branson, Missouri for three days of Osmond Brothers, Mel Tillis and Andy Williams concerts. Joey has a big heart and a head for business.

Wisely, Sally decides to confide in Joey regarding her new painting business.

"I will call it "Wall O' Wonders'!" she tells him.

"Sounds good," Joey responds. "How much are you going to charge for your painting work?" Joey doesn't beat around the bush.

"Well, I called around and the price range for house painters seems to be about $30 per hour. I suppose that is what I'll charge, too," Sally says a bit impatiently. The financial stuff is boring. She feels uncomfortable talking about her prices. It's like the money is a necessary evil. She wishes she could do business without even thinking about money!

"OK," replies Joey. "How much money do you want to make this year?"

"Well, gosh. It seems to me that I could make a TON of money doing these 'faux' finished walls. They are the rage right now!"

"Sally, what is the point of being in business?" Joey asks, going back to basics.

"Well, I can be creative, and helpful to others!" Sally responds enthusiastically.

"You can do that without a business. A business is about making a profit. Taking in more in revenues than you spend on expenses. I am pressing you to confront the questions you don't want to confront...What are you worth? How much money do you deserve? How much money do you want?"

Sally says, "Well, I guess I figured that whatever was leftover at the end of the year is what I deserve."

Joey looks at Sally straight on, eye to eye, and says, "Unless you *plan* otherwise, there will be NOTHING left at the end of the year. I bet the other painters that are charging the going rate don't have anything left at the end of the year. The going rate is only good for going down the drain.

"Sally, you sell your services. Your expertise. Your skill. Your unique touch with a paint brush. You sell *you.* And you have only so many hours a day of you to sell. If you sold a product that could be duplicated a thousand times it would be easier to attach a selling price to that product. We'll talk about selling products later. For now, we need to know how much to charge for *you.*"

"Gosh," Sally replies, "I feel kind of cheap, selling *me.*"

"Look at it this way. Why not make a living doing what you love? You need to bring money into the family cookie jar somehow, right? You were born to paint, to create those wonderful murals, to decorate walls. You are providing a service that no one else on earth can provide. Sure there are others who paint. But no one can duplicate you, but you.

"And when you make your services available to the world, you do the world a great service! What if you only made your talent available once in a while, as a favor, because you don't want to charge for it, because you feel cheap selling yourself? You would spend all day doing something you don't love just for the money. You wouldn't be able to share your talents but for an hour or two, here and there. You would be making a mistake!

"Get over it, Sally. Sell your services. Sell yourself. Make your talents available to folks who are delighted to pay for them. Make a *living* doing what you love."

> *"I'm not the best guitarist in the world. But I am the best at playing* me.*"*
> SHERYL CROW

"Remember Bob Bird from high school? He was that tall, skinny kid with red hair. He was the guy who set the shop class on fire welding a diamond plate steel spice rack! Well, he started a plumbing company called "Eagle Plumbing." He started his business making up selling prices — pulling the numbers out of thin air. Then I gave him the same lecture I am giving you now: figure out how much it costs you to provide your services and charge more than that. Now, Bob is loving his life, and business is booming.

"Before you can set your price, you'll need to learn how to keep score in your company. Read Ellen Rohr's terrific book, *Where Did the Money Go?*. It tells the story of Bob Bird and Eagle

Plumbing. It explains what a Balance Sheet is, what an Income Statement is...and how you use these reports to keep track of the money in your company.

"If you don't have a copy of *Where Did the Money Go?* call Ellen at 877.MAXROHR (877.629.7647) right now and order it, or you can order online at www.maxrohr.com.

I will assume that you've read that book, that you know what financial statements are...the Balance Sheet and the Income Statement as I help you develop a selling price!"

So, Joey becomes Sally's mentor. He helps her figure out how much she should charge for her painting services. Let's follow along and see how they do it!

STEP #1

Find your purpose.

Joey is one of those fortunate folks who does exactly what he wants, every minute of every day. He challenges Sally to do the same.

"Listen, Sally, what is it that you want out of life?"

"What does that have to do with my selling price?" she responds, a bit startled by the question.

"Absolutely everything. There is a great likelihood that you will start this new business and Wall O' Wonders will absolutely take over your life. Your business should serve your life, but most people become a slave to their business. Establish right now what it is you WANT then you can use your business to help you get it.

"I think every person has a purpose in this lifetime. We are each born with inherent skills, genetic gifts and a unique spirit. Discover what your purpose is. When you align yourself with your purpose, everything gets easier, including your business.

"Take some time to reflect on the big questions...Who am I? What am I doing here? What is my purpose? Then we'll talk about selling prices."

ELLEN ROHR'S ABSOLUTELY PAINLESS — FAST-AND-EASY-WHY-NOT-MAKE-YOUR-DREAMS-COME-TRUE PROGRAM.

1. **What is your purpose?** Each of us is given unique talents, genetics and desires. I think it is our responsibility to discover how to use those gifts to be of service to others. What would your life be like if you were absolutely 'on purpose'? (A nice bonus of being 'on purpose' is that you have your greatest chance of being really successful!) When you were a little kid you probably had a very clear idea of what you wanted to be when you grew up. What was that? Is that your purpose? Write it down. If you don't know for sure what the heck your purpose is, that's OK. Keep asking and jot down your hunches. You'll figure it out.

By the way, no fair just thinking through these steps. You must write it down. Committing the thoughts to paper is essential to the program. That's the rule.

> ## *"Don't just think it, ink it!"*
> ### Mark Victor Hansen

2. **Create the Perfect Day.** Write down, in great detail, what your perfect day is like. This is a lot of fun and won't take you but a few minutes. Close your eyes...imagine your perfect day. What time do you wake up? Where? With whom? What do you have for breakfast? Lunch? Dinner? Where do you work? What do you do? How much money do you want to make? To spend? On what? What good works do you want to accomplish? Who would you like to talk to? How much time would you spend outdoors? Alone or with others?

3. **Take stock of your current situation.** Using your perfect day as a guide, write down where you are now compared to where you want to be. What time must you wake up now? Where? With whom? How is your average right-now day different from the perfect day? In some areas, you will be pleased to discover, you are living the perfect day. Maybe your relationships with your kids are exactly what you want them to be. Maybe you absolutely love your home, your job...at least what you have for dinner? In a few areas you might be within spittin' distance of your perfect day. Perhaps you love the work that you do, but your office needs some remodeling. You might find an area where you are way off track. You've discovered that your real purpose is teaching children, but you spend 12 hours a day selling insurance. Just write down the current situation and compare each point to the perfect day.

4. **Pick the area that has the largest variance between what you want and where you are right now.** You don't have to change everything. Just focus on the one point that is farthest from where it should be. That's it. Your energy needs to be focused on narrowing the gap in that one area. For instance, your soul longs for the farming life and you live in an apartment. You pick this area. Now...how to make the changes?

5. **Track your progress with statistics.** Once you've figured out the goal — for instance, a farm in the country — how could you make that happen? How much money would you need? Do you have it? Where could you get it? Do you know which farm or what country? How could you learn about farming? From these questions create a 'to do' list. Wherever possible, assign a number that will keep track of how you are doing. Make yourself talk to three realtors about farm tracts. Statistics keep you honest — you either talked to three realtors, or you didn't. Start a savings account with specific goal of x number of dollars. (That is why I love money. It's so easy to keep score with it!) Get the idea?

6. **Hold yourself accountable.** You are the only one keeping you from the perfect day. Yep. Just you. You are your only obstacle. This is America. The universe is abundant. Get going and make your dreams come true.

"BOOTSTRAPS! EVER HEARD OF 'EM?"

I saw a cartoon once that had the caption: "Self-help books we'd like to see" and there was a book entitled *Bootstraps! Ever heard of 'em?*. Pull yourself up by yours and get going. This little plan for finding your purpose and living your dreams is a good one. It will work. If you are capable of being successful.

What's holding you up? What's in your past that has you in chains, stuck in old patterns of poverty and pity?

You better find out. This book doesn't deal with the spiritual and psychological reasons that keep you from success. There are some wonderful books and resources that can help. Here are a few of my favorites:

> *The Reinvention of Work* by Matthew Fox
>
> *The Soul of the Firm* by C. William Pollard
>
> *The Seven Spiritual Laws of Success* by Deepak Chopra
>
> *The Scientology Handbook* based on the work of L. Ron Hubbard
>
> *Business as a Calling: Work and the Examined Life* by Michael Novak
>
> *Illuminated Prayers* by Marianne Williamson
>
> *The Bible* by you know who

Ultimately, you are in charge of your life. You create your reality. Really. You are not a victim.

> *"When you point your finger, you got three long fingers pointing back at you."*
> MARK KNOPHLER

You can make your dreams come true. It will be challenging. You will have to move upstream. You'll battle insecurity and fear. But why not live exactly how you want to live? Why not make a living doing what you love? Why not?

Sally goes through the Ellen Rohr's absolutely-painless-fast-and-easy-why-not-make-your-dreams-come-true program. Her purpose? First and foremost she wants to be a loving and supportive mother and wife.

She also knows she has been given a creative gift. She loves paint, the feel and smell of it. The sensation of moving it around with a brush. She understands that she offers a unique service when she paints a picture or a wall.

She loves older folks. She had a grandmother who died a few years back. Ever since then she has yearned for her and found great satisfaction helping out at the Senior Center. Joey Paterno introduced her to the group.

And lately she has been intoxicated with the desire to run a successful business. That must be her purpose as well. She writes down her Perfect Day:

> *"I wake up about 7:30 a.m. I'm healthy and happy and thank God for all my blessings! I hug Big Dog and the kids. We have breakfast together on the patio, looking out over the ocean. Everyone takes off for work and school.*
>
> *I check in with my assistant. We have three top-notch wall artists fully booked for the next three months! And my schedule is fun and busy. What a wonderful day: meet with the Joneses to go over their new home plans. Three murals and 'faux finishing' on every other wall. She waited 3 months for me to fit her into my schedule and we are delighted to be working together.*
>
> *Then, a meeting with my accountant and financial planner. I will make over $80,000 this year, after taxes. I am right on target for retiring with $2 million in my retirement accounts. That is in addition to the income-producing properties I own with the kids. Feels great.*
>
> *Next, lunch with a teenager who's presenting me with a business plan. He's got brilliant ideas! I invest in his company with the agreement that he presents financial statements to me every two weeks. We shake hands and he jumps straight into the air and does a back flip.*
>
> *I spend the rest of the afternoon elbow deep in paint creating a mural for the town's new library.*
>
> *Tonight is the Senior Center trip to Cancun. I just love escorting these folks around the world. A few of them need some pretty elaborate equipment to help them get around and it is a pleasure to be able to provide it. Since the Sally Johnson Foundation began, it has donated over $250,000 to the Senior Center for trips and facility improvements.*
>
> *I meet up with Sue and Mike and Big Dog. We have dinner together and plan our trip to Cancun. We laugh, get caught up and relax with each other. I am absolutely in love with my family.*
>
> *What a Perfect Day!"*

When Sally compares her Perfect Day with where she is right now, she realizes that she has a lot of what she really wants. Her family is happy and together. Her health is good, knock on wood. She is confident in her painting skills and she does pitch in at the Senior Center.

The one area in which she is way off is THE MONEY. She has dust in her retirement account. She has $2,000 in her savings account, which she is planning to use to start her new company. She is hand to mouth, month to month with money in and money out. She needs to make changes in the financial area of her life.

The financial area is really — honestly! — easy to improve, compared to other aspects of your life. If your health is poor, or your relationships are in trouble, these are much more serious problems than not having enough money. This is America. You can make money here.

And money lends itself so nicely to statistical analysis. Just count it! How much do you want? How much do you have? How much do you need to live on every month? How much do the things that you want cost? How much do you want to give away? The statistics make the game very clear.

Now...can she create a business that will help her achieve her purpose and live her Perfect Day? YES! And by keeping track of the money it will be easy for her to see what's working and what's not.

She shares this revealing information with Joey.

"Nice work, Sally," he says. "Now, let's figure out how your business can make the money to fuel your dream. Keeping your image of the Perfect Day in mind, start tallying up the costs of operating your business. Some things you need right away and it's easy to figure out the costs. Other expenses, well, you'll have to guess at them. If you lay out your first year of business on paper, before it happens, you can make better decisions when starting out."

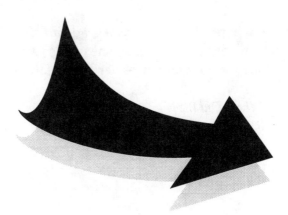

STEP #2

Create a business that will help you serve your purpose.

Your business should serve YOU, not the other way around. Your business is your vehicle for making a living doing what you love.

Sally is convinced that Wall O' Wonders, Inc. is the perfect vehicle for helping her serve her purpose in this lifetime. She has socked away $2,000 for a rainy day. Sally decides to use the $2,000 as operating cash for Wall O' Wonders, Inc.

Spurred on by Joey, she vows to keep meticulous records for her company. Thank goodness for technology. Personal computers make home-based business accounting super easy. She knows that a computer is an absolute necessity and decides to buy one.

She would use all her cash if she chose to buy the computer out right. In her mailbox on any given day, Sally finds 5 or more credit card offers. She is pre-approved, lock-n-load, ready to spend other people's money.   So, what the heck, she figures — charge it!

Sally heads to the Computer Land-O-Megabytes superstore and buys a cool computer with all the bells and whistles. She buys a neat accounting software package to start — from minute one — keeping track of the money. She uses her credit card for the purchase.

She knows she will need a commercial grade airbrush. The airbrush is a nice tool for creating detailed effects in her murals. Really she needs two different styles of airbrushes, but she will settle for just one for now. She uses her credit card to purchase the airbrush.

After reading *Where Did the Money Go?* and looking through the software manual, Sally sets up her Chart of Accounts. Here's what it looks like...

WALL O' WONDERS
4321 Wander Lane
Hometown, USA

CHART OF ACCOUNTS
YEAR 1

1-0000	Assets		
	1-1000	Current Assets	
		1-1110	Checking Account
		1-1140	Petty Cash
		1-1200	Accounts Receivable
		1-1300	Inventory
	1-3000	Fixed Assets	
		1-3100	Equipment
			1-3110 Computer - Original Cost
			1-3115 Computer - Accum Depreciation
			1-3120 Airbrush - Original Cost
			1-3125 Airbrush - Accum Depreciation
2-0000	Liabilities		
	2-1000	Current Liabilities	
		2-1110	Business Credit Card
		2-1200	Accounts Payable
		2-1300	Sales Tax Payable
		2-1400	Payroll Taxes Payable
	2-2000	Long-Term Liabilities	
		2-2100	Bank Loans
3-0000	Equity		
	3-1000	Owner's Equity	
		3-1100	Owner's Investment
		3-1200	Owner's Withdrawal
	3-8000	Retained Earnings	
	3-9000	Current Year Earnings	
4-0000	Sales Income		
	4-2000	Sales - Painting Labor	
	4-4000	Sales - Painting Materials	
5-0000	Direct Costs		
	5-2000	Costs - Sally's Painting Labor	
	5-2010	Costs - Sally's Painting PR Tx	
	5-2050	Costs - Painting Materials	
6-0000	Indirect Costs		
	6-0010	Sally's Owner's Salary	
	6-0011	Sally's Owner's PR Taxes	
	6-0012	Sally's Perks	

continued on next page

WALL O' WONDERS

4321 Wander Lane
Hometown, USA

CHART OF ACCOUNTS
YEAR 1 (CONT'D)

	6-0013	Sally's Retirement Contribution
	6-1100	Accounting Expense
	6-1150	Advertising
	6-1200	Bad Debt
	6-1400	Equipment - Depreciation
	6-1401	Equipment - Replacement
	6-1600	Dues
	6-1700	Entertainment
	6-1800	Insurance
	6-1900	Interest
	6-2295	Lease - Van
	6-2300	Licenses
	6-2400	Maintenance
	6-2500	Office Supplies
	6-2700	Postage
	6-2800	Rent & Utilities
	6-2900	Repairs
	6-4000	Shop Supplies
	6-5200	Telephone
	6-5300	Travel
	6-5400	Uniforms
8-0000	Other Income	
	8-1000	Interest Income
9-0000	Other Expenses	
	9-1000	Interest Expense

Now, Sally will record the first few transactions of Wall O' Wonders, Inc.

▲ She invests $2,000 in the company. This is recorded as Owner's Investment. There is a corresponding entry that shows an increase in assets — the cash in the checking account.

▲ She must account for the purchase of the computer. She'll create a liability and record the new asset — Computer. The cost of the computer is $1,975.

▲ She must account for the purchase of the airbrush. The asset is created, the liability is increased. The cost of the airbrush is $525.

Notice how these transactions are recorded on the Balance Sheet.

Sally invests $2,000 in her business.

WALL O' WONDERS
4321 Wander Lane
Hometown, USA

GENERAL LEDGER
YEAR 1

SRC	Date	ID#	Acct. #	Acct. Name	Debit	Credit	Job
	Day 1			Starts business with $2,000.			
		GJ000001	1-1110	Checking Account	$2,000.00		
			3-1100	Owner's Investment		$2,000.00	
				Grand Total:	$2,000.00	$2,000.00	

WALL O' WONDERS
4321 Wander Lane
Hometown, USA

BALANCE SHEET
DAY 1, YEAR 1

Assets
    Current Assets

Checking Account	$2,000.00		
Total Current Assets		$2,000.00	
Total Assets			$2,000.00

Liabilities

Equity
    Owner's Equity

Owner's Investment	$2,000.00		
Total Owner's Equity		$2,000.00	
Total Equity			$2,000.00
Total Liability & Equity			$2,000.00

Sally buys a computer.

WALL O' WONDERS
4321 Wander Lane
Hometown, USA

GENERAL LEDGER
DAY 1, YEAR 1

SRC	Date	ID#	Acct. #	Acct. Name	Debit	Credit	Job
	Day 1			Buys computer with business credit card.			
		GJ000002	1-3110	Computer-Orig Cost	$1,975.00		
		GJ000002	2-1100	Business Credit Card		$1,975.00	
				Grand Total:	$1,975.00	$1,975.00	

WALL O' WONDERS
4321 Wander Lane
Hometown, USA

BALANCE SHEET
DAY 1, YEAR 1

Assets			
Current Assets			
Checking Account	$2,000.00		
Total Current Assets		$2,000.00	
Fixed Assets			
Equipment			
Computer - Original Cost	$1,975.00		
Total Equipment		$1,975.00	
Total Fixed Assets		$1,975.00	
Total Assets			$3,975.00
Liabilities			
Current Liabilities			
Business Credit Card	$1,975.00		
Total Current Liabilities		$1,975.00	
Total Liabilities			$1,975.00
Equity			
Owner's Equity			
Owner's Investment	$2,000.00		
Total Owner's Equity		$2,000.00	
Total Equity			$2,000.00
Total Liability & Equity			$3,975.00

Sally buys an airbrush.

WALL O' WONDERS
4321 Wander Lane
Hometown, USA

GENERAL JOURNAL
DAY 1, YEAR 1

SRC	Date	ID#	Acct. #	Acct. Name	Debit	Credit	Job
GJ	1/3/99			Buys an airbrush with business credit card.			
		GJ000003	1-3120	Airbrush - Original Cost	$525.00		
		GJ000003	2-1110	Business Credit Card	$525.00		
				Grand Total:	$525.00	$525.00	

WALL O' WONDERS
4321 Wander Lane
Hometown, USA

BALANCE SHEET
DAY 1, YEAR 1

Assets
    Current Assets
        Checking Account $2,000.00
    Total Current Assets $2,000.00
    Fixed Assets
        Equipment
            Computer - Original Cost $1,975.00
            Airbrush - Original Cost $525.00
        Total Equipment $2,500.00
        Total Fixed Assets $2,500.00
    Total Assets $4,500.00

Liabilities
    Current Liabilities
        Business Credit Card $2,500.00
        Total Current Liabilities $2,500.00
    Total Liabilities $2,500.00

Equity
    Owner's Equity
        Owner's Investment $2,000.00
        Total Owner's Equity $2,000.00
        Current Year Earnings $0.00
    Total Equity $2,000.00

Total Liability & Equity $4,500.00

SALLY AND THE 'B' WORD.

Now, Sally knows there will be lots of costs associated with starting and operating her business. She has the accounting software in place to record business activities as they happen — cool!

But to figure out a selling price based on her costs, Sally will have to *guess*. She'll have to do a — I'm going to use the 'B' word, brace yourself — *budget*! Yep, a budget.

I know you hate that word. BUDGET. Everyone does. There is a good reason why: a budget is just a *guess* at what your costs and sales are going to be. It seems like a waste of time.

Think of a budget as a way to write down your goals and hold yourself accountable for them. If you write your goals down, particularly goals that can be attached to numbers and dollars, it makes them so much easier to obtain. The universe just loves for you to ask for what you want! By writing it down, it becomes more powerful.

As she puts her budget together Sally is prone to scrimping. You might be, too. Knock it off. The idea is to make money, not turn into Ebenezer Scrooge.

The idea is not to make the budget as lean as possible. Don't scrimp. Get real.

Sally runs an Income Statement using her accounting software. Because she hasn't sold anything or paid any bills, the Income Statement is all zeroes. A perfect starting point. Using the Income Statement as a guide, Sally will jot a number down on each line from Sales to Net Profit. This budget stuff isn't so bad! These amounts will be her goals for the upcoming first year of business at Wall O' Wonders, Inc.

WALL O' WONDERS
4321 Wander Lane
Hometown, USA

BUDGET WORKSHEET

			% of Sales
Sales Income			
Sales - Painting Labor	$0.00		
Sales - Painting Materials	$0.00		
Total Sales Income		$0.00	
Direct Costs			
Costs - Sally's Painting Labor	$0.00		
Costs - Sally's Painting PR Tx	$0.00		
Costs - Painting Materials	$0.00		
Total Direct Costs		$0.00	
Gross Profit		$0.00	
Indirect Costs			
Sally's Owner's Salary	$0.00		
Sally's Owner's PR Taxes	$0.00		
Sally's Perks	$0.00		
Sally's Retirement Contribution	$0.00		
Accounting Expense	$0.00		
Advertising	$0.00		
Bad Debt	$0.00		
Equipment - Depreciation	$0.00		
Equipment - Replacement	$0.00		
Dues	$0.00		
Entertainment	$0.00		
Insurance	$0.00		
Interest	$0.00		
Lease - Van	$0.00		
Licenses	$0.00		
Maintenance	$0.00		
Office Supplies	$0.00		
Postage	$0.00		
Rent & Utilities	$0.00		
Repairs	$0.00		
Shop Supplies	$0.00		
Telephone	$0.00		
Travel	$0.00		
Uniforms	$0.00		
Total Indirect Costs		$0.00	
Operating Profit		$0.00	
Other Income			
Interest Income	$0.00		
Total Other Income		$0.00	
Other Expenses			
Interest Expenses	$0.00		
Total Other Expenses		$0.00	
Net Profit / (Loss)		$0.00	

Use this space to work out your own budget!

Pretend Dollars vs. Real Dollars

When you create a budget you are working with pretend dollars. You are just writing amounts and $$$ on paper, or clicking them into the budgeting feature of your accounting program.

The numbers you plug into the budget are not the ones you report to the IRS, so you are not bound to make your budget comply with IRS regulations. So, lighten up as you put the budget together. It's pretend. It's what you want to spend in expenses and what you want to create in revenues.

Once the year rolls on, you must use your real dollars to fill out your tax return. You'll submit real numbers on your year-end Balance Sheet and Income Statement.

But the budget is pretend. Have some fun with it and don't worry if you don't know what to put in an account. Take a stab at it, write it down or click it in. At the end of the week, month, year, compare. Match pretend to real and see how far off you are. Then make adjustments.

One of the great things about business — and life — is that when you discover something isn't working, you can change it.

NOTE! Let me explain a few assumptions as we get into budgeting.

1. You are writing down your projected costs (guesses!) for the upcoming accounting period.

2. You'll use these costs to establish what you are going to charge for your services.

3. Then, you'll keep track of your actual costs and sales.

4. You can compare how you really performed with your guesses. The more real data you get, by keeping good records day after day, month after month, year after year, the better your guesses will become. A budget is always a guess. But you will become a better guesser as you keep score with the numbers.

5. You can put items in your budget that are different from the expenses allowed by the IRS. For instance, if you really want to buy a new truck every other year, you can put replacement cost dollars into a budget account.

6. Because of number 5, and because the tax laws are complicated, you'll definitely need an accountant to help you sort out which expenses are deductible and non-deductible.

7. Don't get hung-up on the numbers I use for the illustration. Sally will go through the process so that you understand how it works. Use your own numbers, do your own budget, create your own selling price.

START WITH THE INDIRECT COSTS

Find the Indirect Costs section on the Budget Worksheet on page 25. Figure out how much money you'll probably spend in each of the categories, from Accounting through Uniforms. These are overhead expenses. They are also called indirect expenses as they are indirectly associated with painting. At Wall O' Wonders, Inc., paint and labor to put the paint on the walls are considered direct costs.

Understand that these categories can be customized to fit your business. Sally has Joey help her figure out the accounts. Your accountant may be a good ally as you set up your own chart of accounts.

At this point you might be looking around your home-based office and ask,

"WHAT OVERHEAD?"

Raise your hand if you have ever said, "I can keep my prices low because I don't have much overhead." Hmmmm. I thought so. You can put your hands down now.

First off, let's define the word *overhead*. In business, *overhead* is what it costs you to keep a roof over your head. These costs include rent, insurance, telephone, office supplies...any costs that are not directly associated with a job. Therefore, these costs are also called indirect costs. In contrast, direct costs are directly associated with a job: labor and materials. Direct costs go away when you aren't working on jobs. Overhead bills need to be paid whether or not you are busy.

Overhead also includes the owner's salary, which means the owner is supposed to get paid in slow times as well as busy times.

We usually do a good job of accounting for the direct costs. They are obvious! The overhead costs we tend to discount. Surely, they couldn't amount to much, right?

If you have a small shop, or work out of your home, you might say, "I don't have any overhead!" I am going to ask you not to say that anymore.

Even if you don't pay rent to yourself — in dollars — you still *pay*. Couldn't you use that office as a hobby room, or a private bedroom for one of your kids? Couldn't you line the room with novels and call it a library? Don't you *pay* for dedicating that room to the business? How about the tools, the phone, the cash, or the bank loan? If you access your personal stash to run the business, don't you *pay*?

Does your spouse work with you in the business? Does she (or he) work for free? Does she make sacrifices...all the work and hassle of keeping the business running? Believe me, your family *pays*.

To be fair, you ought to account for those costs. If you ever want to move the business out of your home, or to more spacious digs, pay yourself rent. Before she leaves you, pay your wife a salary. Keep track of your personal contributions and pay yourself back for tools and supplies. Pay yourself a professional salary.

Add up all the real costs of running a business. And charge a price that will cover all those costs plus generate a solid double-digit profit for the company. Don't sacrifice everything for the sake of keeping your selling prices low. Because, when you compromise yourself and your family's well-being for the sake of your customers' wallets, something nasty happens. You start treating your customers like dirt.

When you make a great living doing the wonderful work that you do, something marvelous happens: you treat your customers like gold! You thank them for providing you with such a nice living. You go out of your way to do nice things for them, to make sure they are comfortable.

Understand that overhead costs are significant, no matter how small a business you have. Learn how to create a selling price based on your costs, and then dig in your heels and stick to that price. Your customers want your love and good care...not your lowest price.

LET'S GET TO WORK ON THE BUDGET...

Did you find the section that begins with Indirect Costs? That's where we'll start. For just a moment, Sally will bypass...
  Sally's Owner's Salary
  Sally's Owner's Salary Payroll Taxes
  Sally's Perks
and Sally's Retirement Contributions. We'll come back to these accounts after we fill in the rest of the indirect costs. Hang tight.

Sally goes down each item in the Indirect Costs section, from Accounting to Uniforms, and plugs in a dollar amount. Here is her reasoning behind each item...

Accounting Expense Joey wisely encourages Sally to enlist the services of a professional tax accountant. The tax codes are far too complicated for the average person to comprehend. And Sally wants to paint and manage her business, not fuss over tax rules and regulations. An initial consultation meeting might cost $370, monthly overview of financials and tax filing services...perhaps $100 per month. Sally plugs in $1,570 for accounting expense for year one of Wall O' Wonders, Inc.

Advertising Sally will print up some flyers right off the bat — about $100. And she'll need nice business cards. She's an artist! $300. The van needs lettering. That'll be $800. And then, $30 per month to run a Penny Power ad. Total for year one: $1,520.

Bad Debt Someone is bound to go nuts, or bankrupt, at some point in time. Budget in $600 for the year. Yeah, I know you don't want to factor in any negative stuff but it's real. It happens. Budget for it. *(In fact, when you learn how correct selling prices are created, you'll understand that every expense generates profit! You'll make money on your bad debt. Stay tuned!)*

Equipment - Depreciation Some assets are considered *depreciating assets*. Like your trucks and computer equipment. Over the course of a few years, a truck will rust away, fall apart...eventually be worthless. The IRS understands this and allows you to depreciate, lessen the value of, certain assets by expensing a portion of the asset every year. You record a depreciation expense, but no real dollars are spent at this time. Sally will depreciate the computer and the airbrush over 5 years. She'll budget in $500 for this year's depreciation expense. ($1,975 plus $525 divided by 5 years = $500 per year.) The idea is that you would save that money to use to purchase a new piece of equipment in the future.

But here's the rub: you can only expense the purchase price of the equipment. What would it take to replace the equipment? Take a truck, for instance. In five years, could you replace your truck for the same price?? No! In five years a $20,000 truck might cost $30,000. To record dollars needed to replace or upgrade equipment, you can use a budget account called...

Equipment - Replacement In Sally's case, Sally really needs an additional airbrush to do more intricate mural work. And she would like to be able to upgrade her computer system within the next couple of years. She will include $1,395 in her budget to plan for those purchases, $1,000 for a new air brush, $395 for computer upgrades.

Dues When you set really great goals for yourself, you will frighten a lot of folks around you. Others in your industry will tell you, "You can't charge that much. No one will pay that!" You will start to doubt yourself. It's important that you find and associate with other people who have big dreams and high aspirations. Seek out and join a progressive business association.

Sally learns of an association of artists and designers. It's a national group that meets once a year to share business strategies. The group's mission is to help its members become more profitable. Sally figures she could learn from a group like this and signs up. The yearly dues are $600.

Entertainment You must take out a client or vendor to dinner once in a while. It's only polite. Folks notice when you never pick up the lunch tab. Budget in some money to say, "Thanks for joining me to discuss business today. This one's on me." Sally budgets $600 for entertainment expenses for the year.

Insurance To be fully insured — medical, dental, disability, liability, workers' compensation, life insurance, homeowner's — requires a large premium. But as a self-employed person, who will provide the insurance if not you? It's astonishing how many folks are self-employed and under-insured and justify that they can't afford insurance. They put themselves and their families at risk so that their customers can save money. That's not OK. You can't afford not to be well insured. Insurance is a legitimate business expense and a reasonable compensation expectation. You deserve to be insured. Your family deserves it. Plug in realistic numbers here.

Sally is in denial about insurance. She is depending on Big Dog's government package to cover her family. She puts a measly $1,695 in her budget for insurance, for her vehicle and general business liability. Let's let it go for now and see what unfolds.

Interest When you have loans, you have interest expense. Anticipate how much you'll spend in interest on borrowed dollars and plug the amount into your budget. Sally has $2,500 on her business credit card. At 18%, she'll pay $450 in interest this year. So she puts that amount in the budget.

Lease-Van Sally opted to lease a van for her painting vehicle. Her lease payment is $210 per month, $2,520 for the year.

If you were to buy a vehicle, it would be recorded as an asset on the Balance Sheet. Then, you would expense it via depreciation expense over the course of a few years. Your accountant can help you with the depreciation calculations. If you lease a vehicle, you don't own it, so it's not listed as an asset on the Balance Sheet. But you can expense the entire lease payment. Again, seek your accountant's advice when making the lease or buy decision.

Licenses Sally needs a business license. $75.

Maintenance It takes money to keep equipment in peak operating form. And regular maintenance can save you from costly repairs. Sally estimates $30 for a once a quarter car wash and oil change. Plus a bit more for general maintenance needs that crop up...$360 total for the year.

Office Supplies To get her home office organized Sally figures it will take about $175 for paper, invoices, pens and pencils, file organizers, etc. Then, she budgets $80 a month for the remainder of the year. Total: $1,055.

Postage A roll of stamps every other month? Sounds reasonable. $190.

Rent & Utilities As a home-based businessperson, there are lots of rules regarding rent and utilities expenses. Have your accountant give you a hand with this. Remember, the legal deductions don't affect your budget. You can put whatever you want into your budget, and base your selling price on those numbers. At year's end you will only be able to legitimately expense so much of the actual dollars spent on rent.

Sally figures that one-fifth of her house will be devoted to her business (one room of her five-room house). So she takes 20% of her house payment and 20% of her utilities and calculates a yearly rent & utilities expense of $2,580.

Sally could charge more for the rent of her home. Sure, you're thinking, isn't she robbing Peter to pay Paul if she is just paying the rent to herself? No. Here's the reasoning: the company should be viewed, from square one, as a separate entity. The company needs to pay its own way in the world. Suppose Sally wanted to move the business out of her home someday. How much could the company expect to pay for a commercial space? Sally could plug that figure into her budget. Then, when she decided to move the company from her home, she is already pricing her services with that expense included.

Repairs Stuff happens. No company on earth ever went a whole year without something breaking. So, count on an "ooops" and budget in some money for repairs. Sally has a $500 deductible on her van insurance. In case of a fender bender, she plugs in $500.

Shop Supplies Broom, rags, cleaning supplies, brushes. Hmmm. Sally decides that $85 per month should cover shop supplies.

Telephone Sally's basic phone service is $50 per month. Add in $20 per month long distance for $840 for the year.

Travel Sally wants to attend the national convention of the Artists and Designers Association. This year's keynote speaker is a 'faux finishing' expert and the convention theme is "Be-Faux and After!" How can she miss this?? Her plane ticket will cost $350. Two nights in the hotel will be $300. $140 should cover food, cab fares and tips. She budgets $790 for travel.

Uniforms Land's End catalog has a nice corporate sales division. Sally wants to have shirts and smocks made up with the Wall O' Wonders, Inc. logo. Very professional. The cost will be $130.

All those expenses total $19,000.00 Those are estimates, guesses, of Wall O' Wonders' forthcoming expenses. Some guesses are based on pretty accurate data. For instance, she knows how much the van lease is going to be. Other estimates are pulled from thin air. Like maintenance and shop supplies.

Look over Sally's list of expenses. So far, she has budgeted in $19,000 for indirect costs. Is there anything that is way out of line? Overall she has been **conservative** in her predictions.

The point is not to be too cheap, or wasteful. There is a perfect amount for each of these accounts as determined by what you need and what you want.

You get the idea? Go ahead and do your own. You could keep notes like Sally did to remind you of why you put the number you did in each line in the budget. Later when you compare the real vs. budgeted numbers you might ask yourself, "What was I thinking?" You'll find it useful if you have notes that explain your reasoning.

Now, let's follow Sally to the next step in the process of creating a selling price....

WALL O' WONDERS
4321 Wander Lane
Hometown, USA

BUDGET –
INCLUDING INDIRECT COSTS / OVERHEAD

	Budgeted	% of Sales
Sales Income		
Sales - Painting Labor	$0.00	
Sales - Painting Materials	$0.00	
Total Sales Income	$0.00	
Direct Costs		
Costs - Sally's Painting Labor	$0.00	
Costs - Sally's Painting PR Tx	$0.00	
Costs - Painting Materials	$0.00	
Total Direct Costs	$0.00	
Gross Profit	$0.00	
Indirect Costs		
Sally's Owner's Salary	$0.00	
Sally's Owner's PR Taxes	$0.00	
Sally's Perks	$0.00	
Sally's Retirement Contribution	$0.00	
Accounting Expense	$1,570.00	
Advertising	$1,530.00	
Bad Debt	$600.00	
Equipment - Depreciation	$500.00	
Equipment - Replacement	$1,395.00	
Dues	$600.00	
Entertainment	$600.00	
Insurance	$1,695.00	
Interest	$450.00	
Lease - Van	$2,520.00	
Licenses	$75.00	
Maintenance	$360.00	
Office Supplies	$1,055.00	
Postage	$190.00	
Rent & Utilities	$2,580.00	
Repairs	$500.00	
Shop Supplies	$1,020.00	
Telephone	$840.00	
Travel	$790.00	
Uniforms	$130.00	
Total Indirect Costs	$19,000.00	
Operating Profit	($19,000.00)	
Other Income		
Other Expenses		
Net Profit / (Loss)	($19,000.00)	

How much money do you need and want to fulfill your purpose?

This is an incredibly powerful and frightening question. How much do you want? In dollars. How much do you need, not just to get by but to do all the wonderful things you want to do in your perfect day?

You see, the universe is abundant. If you want the moon and the stars, ask for it. Money just passes through you. You can't take it with you. Whatever wealth you create is an opportunity for you to pass it on, do some good, create new and wonderful things and experiences.

If I was holding a lighted candle, and I reached out to you and set your candle wick on fire, my candle flame would be undiminished. We would now have two burning candles and we could light the whole world on fire! There is enough in this world to go around because we can create whatever we need. We are that powerful, particularly if we are aligned with our God-given purpose.

Would you be a good steward of riches? Then ask for as much as you need, as much as you want.

HOW MUCH SALARY DO YOU DESERVE? DO YOU *WANT*?

What Are You Worth? What price would you put on the gift of life? Priceless? Beyond measure? No way to put that value in dollars?

But we attach a price tag to ourselves every day. How much do you charge for an hour of your life? How much for your knowledge, experience, physical and technical skills? What are you worth?

Once upon a time, Pablo Picasso was sketching in the park when a bold woman approached him.

"Oh, you must sketch my portrait! I insist. Of course I will pay you for it."

So, Pablo agreed to sketch her. He flipped to a fresh page in his sketch book. After studying her for a moment, Pablo used a single pencil stroke to create her portrait. He handed the women his work of art.

"It is perfect!" she gushed. "You managed to capture my very essence with one stroke, in one moment. Thank you! How much do I owe you?"

"Five thousand dollars," the artist replied.

"B-b-b-but, what??" the woman sputtered like a teapot. "But, how could you want so much money for this picture?? It only took you a second to draw this!"

To which Pablo responded, "Madame, it took me my entire life."

How much are you worth?

Let's work through a little exercise that will help you figure out what you're worth. The work you do takes time. And time is the most precious resource. Time reflects your life, sands through the hourglass. When you exchange your time, your life, to go to work, you should be justly compensated. How much do you need to charge to make this business *business* worth your while?

Sally meets Joey for lunch and shows him her budget so far.

"Cool!" he says. "It is a bit conservative but you've covered the basic expenses. Well done. Now comes the scary part. Sally, how much money do you want to make this year? We are going to do a little exercise together to help you figure out exactly how much you want to make this year."

Now, follow along and fill in the blanks as we go.

For one year of your life...

1. How much money do you **need** to pay all your bills?_____

   *This is the bare bones $$ amount. Feed, clothe and shelter your immediate family. Hmmm. Sally plugs in $30,000 for this number. Of course, **your** answer will depend on your definition of bare bones. There is no right answer!! I'll just plug in Sally's numbers as we go along so you can follow the math as you read.*

2. How much more money would make life much more satisfying, make it easier to sleep at night? How much do you **really** want? _____

   How about another $30,000? Life would start to get fun with $60,000 take home pay for the Johnson family, yes? After all, if bare bones was OK, why would you be in business for yourself? You could find a job with less risk and better hours!

3. How much money would you like to contribute to worthy causes? _____

    You know, if you don't support the good causes, who will? This is your responsibility, so pony up! Let's use a very modest $3,000 for Sally's tithing contribution.

4. What do you need to contribute to your retirement fund for the year?_____

    How does your back feel? Are your knees snap, crackle, popping? If you are forty years old and do physical labor you are on borrowed time.   If you don't have a retirement fund started (most folks don't) you will have to contribute pretty heavily to avoid retiring as a homeless person.

    Say your bare bones per year is $30,000. Assume you retire at 55 and live to be 75. 20 x $30,000 is $600,000. That's the bare bones level. Is that what you want? Wouldn't it be nice to retire with $2 million in your retirement funds? How is it going to get there? A financial advisor can map out a savings plan for you. I haven't bothered with details like interest and inflation — this is a quick and dirty formula. But can you see that you must create the money now? Otherwise, you'll be living where you don't want to live and driving what you don't want to drive.

    Sally puts down $12,000 for this year's contribution. She can work with her accountant and financial planner to set up a company funded pension plan. Starting at age forty with $12,000...Hmmm. See how folks resort to buying lottery tickets? There's not much you can do to create an adequate retirement fund if you start saving as an old person. Start NOW.

6. What else? College funds for the kids? Major orthodontia? Weddings and Bar Mitzvahs? _____

    College is just a heartbeat away. And a wedding someday! A big shindig can set you back. Sally puts in $5,000.

OK, let's total up the salary, perks and retirement you need to live the way you want to live.

$_____

Sally's dollars add up to $80,000. $60,000 in pay and $12,000 in retirement and $8,000 in perks, extra dollars for her to spend and give away.

Sally isn't greedy. The CEO of Coca Cola makes about $100 million per year. She could be greedier!

Joey comments, "You know Sally, in your Perfect Day you are a wealthy woman. You aren't overdoing your compensation this year at $80,000. You want to add anything else?

"How many people on this planet know the things that you do? Significantly less than 1% of the world's population can finish a wall like you can. Man, we should be carrying you around on a silver platter! How about a rare-and-useful knowledge bonus?

"Is there anyone outside your immediate family that may need your financial support? How much for them? Aging parents, disabled relatives...that's what families are for."

Sally holds up her hands. "Joey, let's stop right here. Let me use these numbers for year one of Wall O' Wonders. I'll look at the financial statements every month. I'll track all the numbers. If I hit $80,000 in total compensation this first year, I'll be delighted. Then, I promise, I'll raise it for next year. Deal?"

"OK, it's a deal," Joey agrees. "Now, we still have to come up with your selling price! You've assembled your budget of anticipated overhead expenses. And you want to make $60,000 in pay this coming year, plus $12,000 in retirement contributions and $8,000 in perks, extra dollars to spend and give away. You're establishing the cost basis for your selling price. Great.

"Sally, you sell a painting service, a service that is dependent on your time. How many hours do you have to sell? How many hours will you spend on the other tasks needed to operate the business? You can find out by filling out a timesheet."

You could fill out a timesheet, too. Here's a sample form:

TIMESHEET

Name _____

Day _____ Date _____

Activity	Customer	Hours	Billable?

Total # of non-billable hours = _____
Total # of billable hours = _____
Total # of hours worked = _____

STEP #4

How many billable hours can you create?

You are limited in the number of hours that you have in a day, a week, a month, a year or a lifetime to sell those services.

If you were to sell a product like fortune cookies or paper airplanes you could, theoretically, manufacture an unlimited number of cookies and airplanes to sell. When you sell a service that requires your time and your personal skills you are selling something much more precious.

How much time do you have to sell? How many billable hours can you create? The hours for which you are *able to bill* the customer are called **billable hours**.

Sally sells her *time*, her ability to create a magical wall mural or a beautiful, multi-hued wall finish. How many billable hours could Sally generate?

FILL OUT A PRETEND TIMECARD.

If your company is already up and running, great. Use a timecard to record the actual hours spent doing each task that needs doing at your company. If you are just starting up or just considering starting a business, fill out a pretend timecard.

Sally imagines a typical day in her business and jots down the hours.

Name: Sally Johnson		Date: Typical
Hours	Activity	Billable??
2	running for supplies	no
1	computer, paperwork	no
4	painting and finishing	yes
1	phone, bids	no

Now, Sally doesn't want to work more than 40 hours a week. I know, I know. She will! But the point is NOT to run yourself ragged. Let's assume she will keep it to 40 hours a week. If this is a typical day, Sally will spend 50% of her time doing administrative duties — non-billable. And 50% of her time will be billable — the painting and finishing.

All of Sally's time is forwarded to the customer. The running for supplies, the computer and paperwork and the phone and bid tasks are indirect costs that can't be attributed to any one customer. These costs will go into overhead.

The painting and finishing hours will be billed directly to a specific customer. The costs that are incurred for labor and material on a specific job are the direct costs.

The overhead costs and the direct costs will be attached to the billable hour to create a selling price for a billable hour. You'll learn how to create a selling price that covers all the costs of doing business. Hang in there!

Let's figure out the number of billable hours Sally will have over the course of a year.

Billable hours for a typical day = 4.

4 times 5 days = 20 billable hours a week.

20 times 50 weeks a year (Sally wants to take two weeks off for a vacation.)

= 1,000 billable hours per year.

Do you think that looks like too small of a number? It may be, depending on the service you provide. But, people tend to grossly overestimate the amount of billable hours that they can generate. Remember, stuff happens. The dog gets loose, the tire goes flat, the customer isn't home. And all the administrative tasks need to get done.

The only way to know how many billable hours you create is to track the actual data. For now, Sally is guessing 1,000 billable hours. And that is a reasonable number of billable hours for a service provider.

Sally is guessing at these numbers. But, by next month she will have a whole month's worth of real data regarding dollars and billable hours. **The key to using financial statements to help you succeed is to use them and review them...at least once a month. Once a week is even better. Run a Balance Sheet and an Income Statement. Tally up your timecards. Check the numbers.**

Now that she's decided that half of her time is billable time, let's plug her salary dollars into the budget. Look at the Indirect Costs section of the Income Statement budget. We're going to address these accounts...

> Sally's Owner's Salary
> Sally's Owner's Salary Payroll Taxes
> Sally's Perks
> and Sally's Retirement Contributions

Half of the time, Sally wears the owner's hat and performs administrative duties. Sally will plug in half of her $60,000 desired pay in **Sally's Owner's Salary.** Note the $30,000 next to that account.

Her accountant tells her to budget in about $16,000 for payroll taxes. Half of $16,000 is $8,000. Note the $8,000 that is in the budget for **Sally's Owner's Salary Payroll Taxes.**

The $5,000 for special circumstances and the $3,000 contribution amounts are listed together under **Sally's Perks.** These dollars may be taxable. Sally has budgeted $12,000 in **Sally's Retirement Contributions.** There are tax consequences associated with retirement contributions, too. *Remember, this is just a simple formula. Lots of things can influence your actual tax burden.* That's what accountants are for. Sally will consult with her accountant. Just be aware that taxes always need to be taken into account when assessing your costs of doing business!

Here's how the budget looks with all the indirect costs budgeted in.

WALL O' WONDERS

4321 Wander Lane
Hometown, USA

BUDGET – INDIRECT COSTS / OVERHEAD
INCLUDING OWNER'S COMPENSATION

	Budgeted	% of Sales
Sales Income		
Sales - Painting Labor	$0.00	
Sales - Painting Materials	$0.00	
Total Sales Income	$0.00	
Direct Costs		
Costs - Sally's Painting Labor	$0.00	
Costs - Sally's Painting PR Tx	$0.00	
Costs - Painting Materials	$0.00	
Total Direct Costs	$0.00	
Gross Profit	$0.00	
Indirect Costs		
Sally's Owner's Salary	$30,000.00	
Sally's Owner's PR Taxes	$8,000.00	
Sally's Perks	$8,000.00	
Sally's Retirement Contribution	$12,000.00	
Accounting Expense	$1,570.00	
Advertising	$1,530.00	
Bad Debt	$600.00	
Equipment - Depreciation	$500.00	
Equipment - Replacement	$1,395.00	
Dues	$600.00	
Entertainment	$600.00	
Insurance	$1,695.00	
Interest	$450.00	
Lease - Van	$2,520.00	
Licenses	$75.00	
Maintenance	$360.00	
Office Supplies	$1,055.00	
Postage	$190.00	
Rent & Utilities	$2,580.00	
Repairs	$500.00	
Shop Supplies	$1,020.00	
Telephone	$840.00	
Travel	$790.00	
Uniforms	$130.00	
Total Indirect Costs	$77,000.00	
Operating Profit	($77,000.00)	
Other Income		
Other Expenses		
Net Profit / (Loss)	($77,000.00)	

Still a bit fuzzy on the difference between Indirect and Direct costs?

Direct Costs (a.k.a. Cost of Goods Sold, Cost of Sales or Job Site Expenses): These expenses are *directly* related to a sale. If the sale didn't happen, the expense would not be incurred. Direct costs refers to material, labor costs and permits used at a specific *job site*. Or, the cost of the item you purchased intending to resell it.

If a tool was purchased to be used on a specific job and it was used to the point of complete depreciation on that job, then you would include that tool as a direct cost. If you bought a tool to be used on lots of different jobs it would not be a direct cost. It would be an *Indirect Cost*.

Most business owners understand direct costs and charge their customers enough to cover these costs. It's the indirect costs that get overlooked.

Indirect Costs (a.k.a. Operating Expenses or Overhead): Every expense *other* than the direct costs. These are the costs you need to operate the business every day, to keep a roof *overhead*. They are *indirectly* related to sales. These costs remain fairly constant whether you have lots of sales, or sales are down.

An example of an indirect cost is the telephone bill. If Sally had no sales on a particular day, well, the telephone expense would still be incurred. Indirect costs can't be assigned to a specific job. To what job do you assign the copy machine repairs? Get the idea?

Each selling price should be calculated to include a *portion* of your entire indirect cost's burden. It would not make sense to hit up a single customer for your entire rent payment.

Why is it helpful to separate the indirect costs from the direct costs? As a manager, you need to know how much money it takes to cover indirect costs every month. Busy or slow, indirect costs are racking up, hour by hour. How much does it take to 'crack the nut' each month? Without sales, direct costs go away — no problem. Ah, but not so with the indirect costs...you better know how much you need to run your company.

Indirect costs include owner's salary. Why? Well, the owner is entitled to compensation for the administrative functions he performs in the company. When Sally is painting walls and creating billable hours, she'll be paid. Those wages are direct costs. As the owner-manager Sally needs a salary that compensates her work as a manager. Her owner's salary is an indirect cost.

Now look to the Direct Costs section of the Income Statement budget - Sally's Painting Labor.

Wall O' Wonders will pay Sally for her billable hours. She predicts that half of her time will be spent providing painting services. Let's plug in $30,000 for wearing the "Service Provider's hat." Based on the prediction that she will have 1,000 billable hours, that amounts to $30 per hour for her work as an artist. Let's attach $8,000 in anticipated Payroll taxes for these wages.

So, Sally has plugged in her total compensation of $80,000, split between the "hats" she wears as a "painter" - direct cost, and as the "owner" - indirect costs. She even accounted for the tax burden. Atta girl!

WHY NOT ONE LUMP SUM AMOUNT FOR SALLY'S COMPENSATION?

It's important that Sally split her time and compensation up to reflect the direct costs and indirect costs. When she wears the hat of painter we need accurate data for direct costs. How many billable hours did she generate? How much did she make in sales? If she were to lump all the data together, she wouldn't get a clear picture of the billable hours and the costs associated with them. She is setting the stage for future painters.

Play the game straight and separate your direct costs from your indirect costs, even if you are a one person shop. You might want to be a 10 person shop. Lay a good foundation for financial analysis and productivity tracking.

Isn't Sally doing a nice job with this budget? She has all her direct costs for labor and all her indirect costs plugged in. And she has determined that she will base her prices on 1,000 billable hours this year.

How are you doing with your budget? Be sure to fill in your own numbers before we press on.

WALL O' WONDERS

4321 Wander Lane
Hometown, USA

BUDGET – INDIRECT COSTS / OVERHEAD WITH OWNER'S COMPENSATION AND DIRECT COST OF LABOR

	Budgeted	% of Sales
Sales Income		
Sales - Painting Labor	$0.00	
Sales - Painting Materials	$0.00	
Total Sales Income	$0.00	
Direct Costs		
Costs - Sally's Painting Labor	$30,000.00	
Costs - Sally's Painting PR Tx	$8,000.00	
Costs - Painting Materials	$0.00	
Total Direct Costs	$38,000.00	
Gross Profit	($38,000.00)	
Indirect Costs		
Sally's Owner's Salary	$30,000.00	
Sally's Owner's PR Taxes	$8,000.00	
Sally's Perks	$8,000.00	
Sally's Retirement Contribution	$12,000.00	
Accounting Expense	$1,570.00	
Advertising	$1,530.00	
Bad Debt	$600.00	
Equipment - Depreciation	$500.00	
Equipment - Replacement	$1,395.00	
Dues	$600.00	
Entertainment	$600.00	
Insurance	$1,695.00	
Interest	$450.00	
Lease - Van	$2,520.00	
Licenses	$75.00	
Maintenance	$360.00	
Office Supplies	$1,055.00	
Postage	$190.00	
Rent & Utilities	$2,580.00	
Repairs	$500.00	
Shop Supplies	$1,020.00	
Telephone	$840.00	
Travel	$790.00	
Uniforms	$130.00	
Total Indirect Costs	$77,000.00	
Operating Profit	($115,000.00)	
Other Income		
Other Expenses		
Net Profit / (Loss)	($115,000.00)	

Uncle Sam takes all my money!!

I got this letter the other day....

> *Dear Ellen,*
>
> *I had a pretty good year! My Income Statement showed 10% profits, about $40,000.00. But I just learned from my accountant that I owe more than $12,000 in taxes and that doesn't include the money I need to cough up to cover payroll taxes.*
>
> *How can a businessman get ahead when Uncle Sam takes so much of what I bring in??*
>
> *Signed, Fed Up*

Dear Fed Up,

Most Income Statements are formatted to show the bottom line as 'Profits Before Taxes'. This is because your accountant will use whatever shows up on this line to calculate how much tax you need to pay. The problem is, when you look at the Income Statement before your accountant figures the tax amount due, you think you have more money than you really have.

Now, we could argue about the U.S. tax system. And we could choose to lobby and vote and run for office — that's what it would take to change the current tax system. *But in the meantime*, the tax system is what it is. As a citizen and business owner, you are required to deliver taxes to Uncle Sam. And even with its problems, the USA is the absolute best business environment in the world.

Here's the big question: Who pays the taxes? *Your customer.* Taxes are a real cost of doing business. Include taxes as a cost when you do your budget. Create a selling price that will give you solid profits *after* taxes are paid.

As Sally sets up her budget, she'll plug in amounts for payroll taxes. She'll have taxes to pay on the company's income as well. When she sets a selling price, she must plan on those taxes and create a pre-tax income that leaves her with what she wants once taxes are taken out.

STEP # 5

How much should you charge?

Set a selling price that allows you to serve your purpose. Sally sells time, her expertise. She sells billable hours. And she's decided that she'll budget for 1,000 billable hours in her first year of operating Wall O' Wonders, Inc.

The costs of operating Wall O' Wonders must be recouped by the selling price of those 1,000 billable hours. In business jargon, Sally's widget is the billable hour. The billable hour is the labor hour that is directly billed to the customer. Look at Sally's numbers, then fill in *your* numbers.

CREATING A SELLING PRICE FOR ONE HOUR OF LABOR.

1. Find your break-even amount.

Sally has budgeted her direct costs and indirect costs:

Direct Costs =	$38,000
Indirect (Overhead) Costs =	$77,000
Break-even =	**$115,000**

Total costs equal break-even.

What's your break-even?

Direct Costs =	$_____
Indirect (Overhead) Costs =	$_____
Break-even =	$_____

2. Find your break-even amount per billable hour.

$$\frac{\text{Break-even}}{\text{Number of billable hours}}$$

Divide the break-even dollar amount by the number of billable hours you have in a given time period. Sally has a break-even figure of $115,000 for one year, and 1,000 billable hours in one year.

$$\frac{\$115,000 \text{ (break-even)}}{1,000 \text{ (billable hours)}}$$

Sally's break-even for one billable hour is $115. If she generates 1,000 billable hours and charges $115 for each billable hour she will generate $115,000 in sales. At this point she will just break-even for the year. Then, Sally's Income Statement for the year would look like this:

Sales	$115,000	100%
– Direct Costs	$ 38,000	33%
Gross Margin	$77,000	67%
– Indirect Costs	$77,000	67%
Profit	0	0%

What's your break-even per billable hour?

$$\frac{\text{Break-even}}{\text{number of billable hours}} = \$_____$$

3. Determine your desired profit margin.

To create a selling price, inflate the break-even amount to create a profit margin. **The profit margin is the percent difference between break-even and the selling price.** For example, if your break-even for the billable hour is $200 and your selling price for the billable hour is $300, your profit is $100 and your profit margin is 33% ($100 is 33% of sales).

At break-even the profit margin is 0%.

How much profit would you like to make? Remember the profit amount at this point must be generous enough to hand Uncle Sam his share and still leave enough for you. How much is enough? You must decide for yourself. But let me share a little story...

> *Not long ago, I attended my 20-year high school reunion. I was catching up with friends, doing the usual chit chat, "Did you marry that knucklehead you were dating senior year? Whatever happened to Mary Lynn Breckworth? Is she still in prison?" And of course, the classic icebreaking question, " What line of work are you in?"*
>
> *I hadn't seen Helen since our graduation party. She told me she worked in human resources for one of the big financial investment companies.*
>
> *"Wow," I said, impressed. "That must be an interesting job. Do you love it?"*
>
> *"Well, it can be a lot of fun,' Helen sighed, "but recently the company's had some financial problems. Once profit levels hit a certain low level, the whole company goes into 'emergency' mode. It's been a bit stressful. All the belts are tightened and the sales force is put in high gear."*

Now, in the plumbing industry, the average net profit is 1-3%. I know contractors who would give their right eye for 10% bottom line. I was intrigued to know what profit level constituted an 'emergency'. So I asked her.

Helen replied, "Twenty-two percent".

This company considers 22% absolute bare bottom profits. McDonald's aims for 25% or better profits. And I have seen electronics companies and pharmecuetical companies with profit margins of well over 50%.

I bet you were going to plug in 10%, weren't you? Well, Sally was too. Until Joey straightened her out.

"Sally, 10% won't cut it. You need profits to grow your company."

"But Joey, even at break-even, I have paid myself...for my hours wearing the painter's hat and for my administrative role. What do I need the profits for? I don't want to be greedy."

"Sally, the company needs a profit just like you need a salary. The company is an entity separate from you. Profit fuels your company's growth. Remember you need to upgrade your computer and buy another airbrush. What about hiring another painter? He or she will need a van. Do you want to move the business out of the house someday? If you choose to buy a new building, or buy a company to do wallpapering work, you can finance the company's growth with profit. If you were to borrow money to expand more rapidly, your investor would require a return on investment for his risk and exposure. That comes from profits. Make sense? Also, as you grow you could share profits with your employees. Cool, huh?

"Your salary compensates *you* for the headache, heartache, time, risk and energy you put into the company. Your salary provides for you and your family. You need BOTH profit and salary.

"So Sally, how much profit do you want to create?"

Sally settles on 20% pre-tax profit margin. Joey thinks it is too conservative.

What profit margin are you going to create? _____

4. Create a selling price for one billable hour.

Sally wants to create a 20% profit margin. That 20% will be reflected on the bottom line of the Income Statement. We know the dollar amounts of our direct and indirect costs. This is how the Income Statement reflects this information.

Sales for one billable hour	???	100%
– Direct Costs	$38	??%
Gross Margin	??	??%
– Indirect Costs	$77	??%
Profit	??	20%

So, selling price for one billable hour is 100%. Sally's desired profit is 20% of the selling price. The indirect costs plus the direct costs = break-even = 80% of the selling price.

(Now you might want to know the proof of the math formula, so I am going to show it to you. If you don't care, that's OK. Just use the formula as it appears on the next page.)

Math using 20% profit margin for example

$$\text{Selling Price} = 100\% \text{ of Selling Price}$$
$$\text{Profit} + \text{Break-even} = \text{Selling Price}$$
$$20\% + 80\% = 100\%$$

Break-even = 80% of Selling Price

$$\frac{\text{Break-even}}{80\%} = \text{Selling Price}$$

or

$$\frac{\text{Break-even}}{.80} = \text{Selling Price}$$

$$\frac{\text{Break-even}}{X} = \text{Selling Price}$$

When X = reciprocal of desired profit percentage.

Reciprocal is the number that added to another number equals 100%. The reciprocal of 20% is 80%. The reciprocal of .20 is .80. You get that? Good work. I bet it hasn't been since high school that you thought about these math concepts. Don't worry — the math won't get any more complicated than this!

Here's the formula for generating a selling price with a 20% profit margin for one billable hour:

$$\frac{\text{Break-even}}{80\%} = \text{Selling price}$$

Remember from high school that 80% and .80 are the same number? You can divide by .80 if you think it's easier to plug into the calculator.

To use Sally's numbers...

$$\frac{\$115}{80\%} = \frac{\$115}{.80} = \$144 \quad \text{(I rounded \$143.75 to make it a simpler number.)}$$

Here's what the Income Statement for the sale of this one billable labor hour would look like:

Sales for one billable hour	$144	100%
– Direct Costs	38	26%
Gross Margin	106	74%
– Indirect Costs	77	54%
Profit	$29	20%

Sally will make $29 profit dollars, 20% of sales, for every billable labor hour she sells for $144.

Plug your numbers into the selling price formula to come up with what you will charge for a single billable labor hour.

$$\frac{\text{Break-even}}{x} = \text{Selling price}$$

Where x is the reciprocal of your desired profit percentage.

You fill in your numbers...

$$\frac{\underline{\hspace{3cm}}}{\underline{\hspace{1.5cm}}} = \$\underline{\hspace{2.5cm}}$$

Congratulations! You have established a selling price for one billable hour of your services. Hang onto that number. We are going to use it to finish our budget.

And keep your break-even per billable hour amount handy. We'll use that number to create in the field selling prices for your services that will make your dreams come true!

GULP.

Is your selling price for the billable labor hour a LOT more than the going rate in your industry? I thought so.

Think you could sell your labor hour for less and make up the difference with material sales?

Let me ask you...is your value to the marketplace your ability to sell material? Or do customers value your ability to assemble, to create, to assess, to think, to install, to paint?

This selling price exercise might scare the pants off you. You might decide that, really, you aren't worth that much. That the hassle of asking for that price is too much. That it would be fine if everyone *else* in your industry realized what they were worth and charged that much.

That's just fear and denial talking. Ignore them and let's keep going!

WAIT A MINUTE!

What if I took my costs and multiplied them by 20%? Using Sally's cost for one billable hour of direct and indirect costs...

$$\$115 \times 20\% = \$23$$

Then I added that dollar amount to my costs.

$$\$115 + \$23 = \$138$$

Wouldn't that give me my selling price with a 20% profit?

NO! And here's why not...

Suppose you created a selling price this way. Then you recorded the transaction for the sale of one billable hour in your accounting program and ran an Income Statement report. This is what you would find...

Sales	$138	100%
- Total costs	115	83%
Profit	$23	17%

This illustrates the difference between *markup* and *margin* — two commonly misunderstood words.

Markup: is a percentage applied to the cost of an item to create a selling price. The problem with using a markup is that the percentage amount of the markup won't equal the percentage amount of profit that you generate. So you will be disappointed at the bottom line, even if your actual costs and sales figures are on budget. And if you are pricing for meager profits in the first place, a markup of a percent or two can result in no profit at all.

Margin: is the percentage difference between cost and selling price. In the above example there is a 20% markup that creates a 17% profit margin.

BACK TO SALLY'S BUDGET....

Let's look at Sally's budget again. She guess-timated that she would generate 1,000 billable hours this first year. If she sells each one at her selling price of $144 per billable hour she will generate labor sales of $144,000.

$144 per billable hour x 1,000 billable hours = $144,000 in total labor sales

See how that amount is added to the Income Statement budget.

Multiply *your* selling price for a billable hour by the number of billable hours you've predicted. Fill in the total labor sales in your budget.

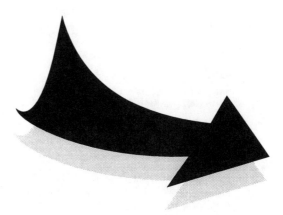

WALL O' WONDERS
4321 Wander Lane
Hometown, USA

BUDGET – INDIRECT COSTS / OVERHEAD WITH OWNER'S COMPENSATION AND DIRECT COST OF LABOR & PROJECTED LABOR SALES

	Budgeted	% of Sales
Sales Income		
Sales - Painting Labor	$144,000.00	100%
Sales - Painting Materials	$0.00	0.0%
Total Sales Income	$144,000.00	100.0%
Direct Costs		
Costs - Sally's Painting Labor	$30,000.00	20.8%
Costs - Sally's Painting PR Tx	$8,000.00	5.6%
Costs - Painting Materials	$0.00	0.0%
Total Direct Costs	$38,000.00	26.4%
Gross Profit	$106,000.00	73.6%
Indirect Costs		
Sally's Owner's Salary	$30,000.00	20.8%
Sally's Owner's PR Taxes	$8,000.00	5.6%
Sally's Perks	$8,000.00	5.6%
Sally's Retirement Contribution	$12,000.00	8.3%
Accounting Expense	$1,570.00	1.1%
Advertising	$1,530.00	1.1%
Bad Debt	$600.00	0.4%
Equipment - Depreciation	$500.00	0.3%
Equipment - Replacement	$1,395.00	0.9%
Dues	$600.00	0.4%
Entertainment	$600.00	0.4%
Insurance	$1,695.00	1.2%
Interest	$450.00	0.3%
Lease - Van	$2,520.00	1.8%
Licenses	$75.00	0.0%
Maintenance	$360.00	0.3%
Office Supplies	$1,055.00	0.7%
Postage	$190.00	0.1%
Rent & Utilities	$2,580.00	1.8%
Repairs	$500.00	0.3%
Shop Supplies	$1,020.00	0.7%
Telephone	$840.00	0.6%
Travel	$790.00	0.5%
Uniforms	$130.00	0.1%
Total Indirect Costs	$77,000.00	53.5%
Operating Profit	$29,000.00	20.1%
Other Income		
Other Expenses		
Net Profit / (Loss)	$29,000.00	20.1%

Now, let's plug in the material sales and costs....

Keep in mind that we have created a selling price for an hour of labor that covers **all the overhead** and direct costs plus includes a profit. DON'T count on the material sale to generate dollars to cover overhead. Why not? Well, if your value to the market is your ability to install, or create, or DO anything, your widget is the labor hour. That's what you sell. You might not get the material sale.

If they were looking for material only would they call you??

Sure, Sally sells paint. But her unique and marketable service is her ability to transform that paint to a wall-bound work of art. If someone asked Sally to buy a gallon of paint, would her can of paint be significantly more valuable than the can at Lowe's or Home Depot or Sam's Club? No. The big stores can whip Sally when it comes to the material only sale.

But Sally will supply the paint she applies, so let's plug in some numbers for the material costs and sales. Sally figures she will use about 3 gallons a day — based on the amount of paint she uses during four billable hours.

3 gallons/day x 5 days/week x 50 weeks/year = 750 gallons

The average cost of a gallon of paint is $18

750 gallons x $18 = $13,500

She plugs $13,500 into Direct Costs — painting materials

All costs generate profit dollars. Sally creates a 20% profit margin for the paint.

$$\frac{\$13,500}{.80} = \$16,875$$

She puts $16,875 in the budget under Sales - painting material. Now, you need to go through a similar process to estimate and budget for your material sales. Remember that the overhead costs are covered in the selling price for the billable hour. You just need to estimate the direct costs of the materials and put it in. Then create your desired profit margin on materials and plug it into the material sales line on the budget.

Check out the numbers on Sally's budget Income Statement.

WALL O' WONDERS
4321 Wander Lane
Hometown, USA

BUDGET
INCLUDING ALL INDIRECT COSTS, DIRECT COSTS, AND PROJECTED LABOR & MATERIAL SALES

	Budgeted	% of Sales
Sales Income		
Sales - Painting Labor	$144,000.00	89.5%
Sales - Painting Materials	$16,875.00	10.5%
Total Sales Income	$160,875.00	100.0%
Direct Costs		
Costs - Sally's Painting Labor	$30,000.00	18.7%
Costs - Sally's Painting PR Tx	$8,000.00	4.9%
Costs - Painting Materials	$13,500.00	8.4%
Total Direct Costs	$51,500.00	32.0%
Gross Profit	$109,375.00	68.0%
Indirect Costs		
Sally's Owner's Salary	$30,000.00	18.6%
Sally's Owner's PR Taxes	$8,000.00	4.9%
Sally's Perks	$8,000.00	4.9%
Sally's Retirement Contribution	$12,000.00	7.5%
Accounting Expense	$1,570.00	1.0%
Advertising	$1,530.00	1.0%
Bad Debt	$600.00	0.3%
Equipment - Depreciation	$500.00	0.3%
Equipment - Replacement	$1,395.00	0.8%
Dues	$600.00	0.3%
Entertainment	$600.00	0.3%
Insurance	$1,695.00	1.0%
Interest	$450.00	0.3%
Lease - Van	$2,520.00	1.6%
Licenses	$75.00	0.0%
Maintenance	$360.00	0.2%
Office Supplies	$1,055.00	0.7%
Postage	$190.00	0.1%
Rent & Utilities	$2,580.00	1.6%
Repairs	$500.00	0.3%
Shop Supplies	$1,020.00	0.6%
Telephone	$840.00	0.5%
Travel	$790.00	0.5%
Uniforms	$130.00	0.1%
Total Indirect Costs	$77,000.00	47.9%
Operating Profit	$32,375.00	20.1%
Other Income		
Other Expenses		
Net Profit / (Loss)	$32,375.00	20.1%

HURRAH!! Sally's budget is finished. And yours too, if you are playing it straight and filling in all the numbers. The budget now becomes the benchmark against which she measures her actual performance. It's time for Sally to use her budget to create actual selling prices to present to her customers.

SELLING PRICE FORMULA FOR A LABOR ONLY JOB:

of billable labor hours _____ x Selling price per billable hour $_____ = $_____

For example, suppose a customer bought her own paint already and asks Sally to create a mural. Sally figures it will take her 12 hours to complete the work.

# of billable labor hours 12 x $144 = $1,728 = Selling Price

Isn't this easy??

SELLING PRICE FORMULA FOR ANY JOB:

of billable hours _____ x Break-even per billable hour $_____ = $_____

Materials:_____

_____

_____

Total Cost of Materials: $_____

Any other Direct Costs:_____

Total other Direct Costs: $_____

Break-even for Job: $_____

$\dfrac{\text{Break-even for Job}}{.x}$ = Selling price of job where x = reciprocal of desired profit percentage.

Calculate *your* selling price for a job:

$\dfrac{\$\underline{\quad\quad}\ \text{Break-even}}{\underline{\quad\quad}}$ = $_____ Selling Price

Example: Sally figures a job will take 4 hours and $36 in paint.

# of billable hours _4_ x Break-even per billable hour _$115_ = _$ 460_

Materials: _paint_　　　　　　Total Cost of Materials: _$36_

Break-even for job: _$496_

Create selling price for 20% profit . . .

$\dfrac{\$496}{.80}$ = $620 = Selling Price

The higher the costs the more profit you make.

Notice that the higher your costs the more profit you generate. Every cost you have generates profit dollars. This isn't wrong. It's standard accounting.

Remember bad debt expense? Bad debt is a legitimate cost of doing business. Sally budgeted in an anticipated amount of money that a customer might refuse to cough up for services rendered. It happens. Well, Sally actually generates profit from that expense.

And that's a good thing to remember as Sally goes to work. Even if someone dies and doesn't pay — Sally still makes money. When you make money in your business, when the rewards are commensurate with the headache and risk, then business is fun. And it's really easy to be nice to your customers.

Lawyers, self-esteem and hourly rates.

Imagine how nice it would be if the going rate actually supported a good living. Makes me drool just thinking about it. Lawyers charge by the hour. Even the newest, greenest lawyer will charge well over $100 per hour. Lawyers believe in the value of their services.

Seventy percent of the world's lawyers live and work in the United States. Most of the world has no use for lawyers.

My personal School of Hard Knocks is the plumbing and heating industry. Most of the world enjoys the benefits of plumbing. Good plumbing has saved more lives from death and disease than doctors will ever cure. Plumbers have done such a stellar job of moving safe and clean water into our homes and waste away from our homes that many epidemic illnesses have been virtually eliminated.

For all the jokes about plumbers in Cadillacs, rolling in the dough, the average net profit for a plumbing company is 1.5%! My mentor, Frank Blau, told me why plumbers do so poorly in business.

Frank said, "It's a self-esteem problem...plumbers don't see the valuable work that they do. They don't think they deserve to make a decent living. And until they do, they never will."

When Frank Blau started his plumbing business, he worked primarily in the new construction field. He is a numbers guy and the numbers weren't adding up. He would need to charge four times the going rate to make the salary and profits that he and his employees deserved.

In new construction, plumbing is almost a commodity. Most new construction plumbers are willing to work for peanuts. Frank switched his focus to service plumbing. In this field Frank could differentiate his company. He poured on the good service and customer care. He found that customers were willing to pay more for his services because his technicians are clean and dependable, his call takers are pleasant and the work is done professionally and right away.

Compare that kind of service with the stereotypical plumbing experience...a surly call taker tells the customer that the service technician will be there whenever, the technician never shows and never calls...or the tech shows up, in a dirty pair of jeans with visible butt crack.

What does that stereotype tell you about the self-esteem of the average plumber? That's why he charges less than it costs him to be in business. That's why he tolerates such a low return on his billable hour. He doesn't think he deserves any more than nothing.

And plumbers aren't the only ones who suffer from low self-esteem. Very few of us make it to walking upright without carrying a whole bundle of negativity and criticism. Your lack of wealth is tied to your inability to BE wealthy. As your self-esteem improves, your ability to be wealthy increases.

Realize your worth. Then, you'll be able to charge what you need to make your dreams come true.

THE CASE FOR FLAT RATE.

Sally is understandably nervous about charging $144 per billable hour, especially since her competitors are charging an average of $30. No one she called charged more than $42 per hour. Time to consult Joey.

"Joey, if I tell my customers that I charge $144 per hour, they'll never go for it."

"Sally, let's pretend that I come to your house to give you a price on repairing your computer. I tell you how much I charge per hour. What would you say to me?"

"Hmmm. I guess I'd ask how long it would take you to fix it."

"Why would you ask that?"

"Well, I'd want to know how much it was going to cost."

"Would you rather know how much the repair is going to cost before or after I do the work?"

"I'd want to know how much it would cost before you did the work, of course."

"Sally, what if you gave your customers a total price — up front — to do the mural or wall finishing. Just like you, your customers want to know 'how much'. What if you promised them that you would hold to that price, no matter what, because you know they don't like surprises. What if you took yourself right out of the hourly rate competition by not quoting an hourly rate at all?

"I don't like hourly rates for service. What if another painter quoted an hourly rate of $30, then took five times as long as you would take to do the work? Think about it. The longer you take, the more you get paid. That's not fair. Your customers pay *more* for inefficiency.

"Very few goods and services are sold on an hourly rate basis. When someone quotes me an hourly rate for anything, I always ask, 'Do you know how much it costs you, per hour, to be in business?' I always get an answer that refers to the going rate. But 1 in 100 knows their break-even, budgeted or actual. They are just making these numbers up. Sally, you can't base your selling prices on what your competitors are charging. They just don't have a clue.

"Ninety-nine percent of all services are sold on a flat rate basis. Can you imagine asking a waiter how much per hour the chef charges? Or asking how much per hour to fly from Dallas to Paris? As a customer, you don't really care what the hourly figures are. You just want to know 'how much' for the service. Or the meal. Or the blouse. Or the haircut. Or the new roof.

"When you quote an hourly rate, people confuse what you charge per hour with what you take home in salary or wages. You didn't understand overhead and break-even until just now. Only savvy business people are familiar with those concepts. And I'm telling you, there are not that many savvy business people around! When you quote even $30 per hour, your customer, who makes $10 per hour at his job, thinks you are rolling in the dough. Why even bring it up? Why not quote a flat rate price to provide the whole service, from tip to tail, to their satisfaction?

"And as you key into your unique purpose, you'll discover the unique services that only your company can provide. Then, you'll have folks waiting in line to be your customers!"

Sally took a practice swing...

"Mr. Jones, we don't charge by the hour. I'll spend time with you to discover exactly what you want, and how to make your home wonderful. And then I will present you with several options for creating just the effect you are looking for. I'll provide an exact price for each option, to do the whole job, to your satisfaction. How's that sound?"

"Atta girl, Sally. You're getting it! Have the customer sign off on the price right on the bid. Another major advantage of charging a flat rate, up-front price is that you can collect on the job. You can be a COD company. No more sending out invoices and waiting 60 days for your money. Your customers expect to pay the bill when they have agreed, beforehand and in writing, to the price of your wonderful services."

"I understand what you're saying Joey, but I am still afraid no one will say yes to my prices."

STEP #6

Overcome Denial. Get comfortable with your selling price.

You might go out of business charging a fair price. There is that risk. But there is the absolute certainty that you will go into debt if you persist in offering your services for less than it costs you to create them.

Going out of business is not the worst thing. If something doesn't work, go back to the drawing board. Search your heart. Crunch some pretend numbers. Try again. No problem. That's a fun game.

You know what's a lot worse than going out of business? Blindly pressing on in a sinking business. Tapping into your home equity line, deeper and deeper, to pay your bills. Neglecting to run your financial reports because you are just too darn busy. And then discovering, a few years later, that you are out of borrowing power. You are so upside down, you have to sell your house to avoid bankruptcy. That's a lot worse.

WHAT'S THE POINT?

According to the Association of Home-Based Businesses, 6,000 people a day are starting a home-based business. By the year 2001, half of all homes will have a home-based business. Millions of take-this-job-and-shove-it departure scenes are unfolding as fed-up employees pitch their jobs and set out for independence. Imagine a 30-year-old electrician. He's had it with long hours and meager wages. He quits! Starts *Short and Spark Electrical Company.* The rush of freedom is delightful, and our newly self-employed hero can be heard boasting....

"Yeah, I'm out on my own now. Tired of making my boss rich. He was ripping people off anyway. I'm going to keep my overhead low, and I don't mind working long days. Heck, I'm used to it! My dad taught me to work hard and do right by folks and business will take care of itself."

The negative numbers at the end of year one are chalked up to 'start up' costs. Fair enough.

Year two ends in the red.

"Money isn't all that important. Spending time with my family is top priority."

Year number three shows a $15,000 loss. And our friend tallied over 3,000 hours working in his own business. The phone rings day and night. He isn't even nice anymore when he answers it. He hasn't seen a family member in three days.

Hmmmm.

Hey fella! What if you raise your prices to the point where you make lots of money and work part-time?

"People in my town won't pay those big city prices. Look at old Mrs. Johnson. She practically threw me out of her house when I charged her $50 to run that electrical line to her basement."

That's interesting. I just saw Mrs. Johnson at Best Buy shelling out $1,500 for a new television. She said that remodeled basement is going to be a new game room for the grandkids. Seems folks here pay big city prices for clothes, cars, toys, movies, video games, furniture, and Beanie Babies.

"Every other electrician in town charges $50 an hour. If I charged more than that I would be out of business tomorrow."

Are you better than every other electrician in town?

"Oh yeah. I don't do just any kind of electrical work. Very few people can negotiate a power panel like I can. And I am an electronic specialist."

You do pretty technically advanced work. I bet that you are the only one within 100 miles of here who can do that sort of work. Why couldn't you charge more for your services? People expect to pay more for better quality. That's why a Lexus costs more than a Festiva.

"Not in my town. People here can't afford Lexuses. I can't raise my prices."

Oh look, there's Mrs. Johnson. Check it out! She has at least a dozen Furbies stuffed in her shopping bags. Those things cost $44.95 apiece, can you believe it? Anyway, with all your technical skills, maybe you should work for NASA or the Department of Defense- Stealth Bomber Division. Maybe you are wasting your talents in the home service business.

"Could be. But I really like the freedom of working for myself."

Yeah, I bet that's nice. When was the last time you took a vacation?

"I took Tuesday off last week. I had to go to the doctor to have an MRI done on my back."

Gee, sounds like fun. Let me guess... you don't have any insurance, do you?

"As a self-employed businessman? Are you kidding? Besides, my wife is planning to go back to work once our fourth kid starts kindergarten. The cheese factory has a graveyard shift and a pretty good insurance package."

Super! What if you hired someone to help you? Find a sharp kid fresh out of high school. You could pay him, oh, say at least as much as a Fed Ex driver makes, heap on the benefits and split the work with him.

"I told you, I only do the highest quality work. There's no one out there who can do the kind of highly sophisticated, super secret, learned-it-from-my-dad kind of work that I do."

OK. Well, what if you trained him at the technical schools the manufacturing community offers, sent him off to seminars by the industry gurus and worked with him, side by side, for a year or two?

"I couldn't afford it. Besides, he would probably leave me and start his own business."

Kids these days have a lot of choices. The 'handy' kids, you know, the ones who do really well in shop class, can become computer programmers and work at Microsoft. Hard to woo them to the traditional trades.

"That's the problem with kids today. They want money and benefits and a nice place to go to work. They don't want to crawl under houses and freeze their butts off and pull a 'live wire' every now and then. They want it easy. They're wimps."

Uh huh. How about your retirement, anything put away?

"No, but someday I figure I could sell my company. I have a great reputation as an electrician — my 'goodwill' is worth a lot."

I bet investors are going to line up for Short and Spark Electrical Company. Let's see. You don't make any money. You don't get any time off. No benefits or retirement. And you're not willing to raise your prices. How about pitching this home-based business gig and working for the utility company? I hear that they are a union shop with hefty benefits, including retirement. Or have you considered Nationwide Electrical Company? They're always looking for good workers.

"No way! The utility is trying to run guys like me out of business. And the national consolidators rip people off with their high prices. I'm free, my own boss. How could I give that up?"

Your back is bad. And $50 an hour isn't cutting it. Here's an idea! What if you became a teacher of electrical work? Why don't you teach a class? Or better yet, you could write a book about what you know. That way you could share your knowledge and not break your back!

"There's nothing I hate more than a has-been electrician *selling* his information. Those who can't do, teach...right? I went to a seminar once and the speaker actually sold books and videos in the back of the room. What a schmuck. I mean, he knows that electricians don't have money for that kind of stuff. You think he'd just be honored to have us show up to listen to him!"

But, your knowledge is so impressive. It would be a shame if you didn't pass it on.

"I'd like my son, Tommy, to go into the family business. Hey, if he cuts the mustard, he could start a business for himself, just like his old man."

What an opportunity for Tommy. Speaking of opportunity, maybe you could get involved with a network marketing company like Amway. That way you could have a home-based business and maybe make some extra cash.

"What, me sell something? I'm no salesman. I hate salesmen! I'd rather die than sell stuff for a living."

Good for you. Well, it's a brand new year. How is the new year going to be different than the last three?

"I'm hoping that the economy picks up."

> *"Whether you think you can, or you think you can't, you're right."*
> HENRY FORD

VOW, NOW, TO NEVER BEAT ANYONE UP OVER PRICE EVER AGAIN!

Sally figures she could cut some costs by pressing on her suppliers. If her costs were lower, her prices wouldn't have to be so high.

"John down at Carper's said he could give me another 10% off!" she boasts to Joey.

"Sally, I can't believe this conversation! I am working with you, trying to help you figure out a good selling price for your painting services. We've discussed how expensive it is to run a first-rate service company. You told me that you were going to dig in your heels and charge a price that would reward you for all the risk and headache. Now, you want to torture your main supplier over a gallon of paint?"

Joey shook his head. "You are never going to get top dollar for your services if you never pay more than rock bottom for anything. You can't have it both ways.

"Here's the deal. You figure out your costs of doing business. Be realistic and generous with your estimates as you plug in the budget numbers. And be willing to let your suppliers, vendors, employees and everyone else you work with make a decent living as well.

"When you are shopping for anything, ask the price. Then, politely accept or refuse. You don't have to buy anything, ever. If you don't see the value, don't buy it. But don't haggle.

"Eliminate the word *gouger* from your vocabulary.

"I think everyone has the right to charge whatever they want for their goods and services. And everyone has the right to buy or pass. Really, unless someone has a gun to your head, how can you be 'ripped off'?

"Let folks charge what they want to. Cultivate win-win relationships with all your vendors. If you win and they lose, you will lose as well, soon enough."

Joey pulls out a sheet of paper and asks Sally to agree to the following statement:

I VOW TO NEVER BEAT UP ANYONE OVER PRICE AGAIN. REALLY.

Signed _____*Sally Johnson*_____ **Dated** _*today!*_

Now, you sign it......

I VOW TO NEVER BEAT UP ANYONE OVER PRICE AGAIN. REALLY.

Signed _____ **Dated** _____

"If I do what I love, won't the money follow??"

NO!!

Do What You Love... But mind the MONEY!!

There is a hip business book that raced up the best seller list: *Do What You Love and the Money Will Follow.* Ha! Not true. It's a myth! Doing what you love for a living is wonderful, essential. But the money *won't* necessarily follow. That's why there are starving artists and business owners who work 100 hours a week and make less than minimum wage.

In fact, doing what you love can fool you into thinking the money doesn't matter. Money does matter. You have mouths to feed, taxes to pay, employees who depend on you, charities to support, tithing to contribute...and it all takes money. Money is handy. It's a nice, neutral medium for exchanging goods and services. And it beats trading for chickens.

So, why do so many folks justify their poor financial performance??

"I take pride in my work. I'm not in it for the money."

It drives me nuts when someone says this — for every non-profitable business person will ultimately depend on me and our welfare system to support them. You can do what you love...just make money doing it.

"Put your heart and soul into your work and you're sure to be successful."

There is one way — only one way — to be successful in business: charge more for your products than it costs to create and deliver them. First class customer service and flawless quality are NOT the keys to success. Take more money in than you send out.

Does this all seem self-evident? Then why do so many pussyfoot around this subject? Are you afraid that wanting money makes you a bad guy?? Perhaps, if you are good enough and kind enough money will just drop in your lap as a well deserved reward.

Profits and integrity are not opposites. The barely-getting-by business person never has enough money to contribute to good causes. And the fellow who is pressed for money will compromise his principles much sooner than the fellow with some 'cushion'.

Do what you love, and the money *may* follow...if you confront and manage the financial aspects of your business. It is not enough to hope and pray. You must DO the things that insure your success.

> Once upon a time there was a nice fellow named Louie. Louie was kind, hard working and very religious. He worked hard but had little to show for all his years of service to his community. One day, he walked into a church, fell to his knees and cried out,
>
> "Dear God, I am a good man and I have led a good life. I have never asked you for anything. Please, grant me this one favor. Let me win the lottery. I will ask only for this as long as I live."
>
> Twenty years passed — Louie never won the lottery. Frustrated, Louie cried out to the heavens, "God, why would you not grant me my one and only wish??"
>
> The sky opened, and the voice of God sounded...
>
> "Louie, you gotta buy a ticket!"

Address the financial aspects of your business head-on. Read your financial statements at least once a month, as often as once a day.

Do what you love...but mind the money.

Charge more than it costs you to be in business.

"I'LL PRICE MYSELF OUT OF THE MARKET!"

At this point, Sally has three choices.

❶ She can charge the going rate.

❷ She can change her mind about going into business for herself.

❸ She can go with the selling price she created using her own costs of doing business.

These are your choices as well. Let's look at each one and its implications.

Suppose you charge the going rate. Now, if you have done all the math so far, you know how much it will cost you per hour to be in business. Even if you reduce your owner's compensation, is your break-even point less than the going rate? I thought so. This is why so many small businesses fail. The owners don't have any idea what it's costing them to be in business.

What if you copy your competitor's selling price, a price that has no basis in reality? You might delude yourself into thinking it will work...if you just work harder, longer. You might think that all this math is wrong, it must be, because everyone else is making good money at the going rate. Right? Maybe you are thinking...

"I'LL REDUCE MY OVERHEAD!"

Look back over your list of costs. How could you reduce your overhead costs? Would the power company take less than the amount due on the electricity bill? How about insurance premiums? Maybe you could *steal* the uniforms? Really, who would get stiffed if you decided to significantly cut your overhead?

You. You and your employees. You would take the hit. In salary and benefits. In fact, lots of small business owners never pay themselves. With what? There is no money left at the end of the month. What about retirement? Most self-employed folks don't have a retirement plan. If there is a social security system when you retire, you won't have those benefits unless you've paid into it. You have to pay yourself to be eligible.

Knowledge imposes responsibility. Now that you know your break-even costs, you can't play dumb again. Sorry. How can you charge less than it costs to offer your services, now that you know the numbers?

You will most certainly lose money at the going rate. Is that OK? Because you will take someone down with you as your company flounders. Your spouse, your kids, your suppliers, your customers.

Suppose you don't go into business for yourself. Would that be the worst thing? If you could work for someone else and make a comfortable living, would that be better than sinking every last nickel, and going into debt, to float a business that isn't going to work?

Sure every business is risky. That is part of the adventure. But if you aren't willing to charge a real and reasonable selling price for your services, you best stay out of the business.

It is OK to say, NO to a business opportunity that doesn't work for your life. Your life should be served by your career, by your business. If it doesn't fit, don't wear it.

Suppose you commit to a selling price based on your costs and your desired salary. Just suppose it works! How would that be?? How would it feel to make exactly what you want to make for doing just what you want to do? To fulfill your unique purpose in this lifetime, and be justly — to your definition — compensated for it.

Wouldn't that be cool?! And why not?

Ever hear of a company called FedEx? Now, FedEx is the highest priced courier service in the market. The U.S. postal service offers 1-3 day service for $3. UPS offers a 3 day service for about $8. FedEx is at least 25% higher than UPS. And FedEx is the undisputed number one company in their industry.

How can that be so? Well, because if you *absolutely have to have it overnight*...who are you going to call?

FedEx is the king of the hill because they are BETTER and they TELL YOU about it.

Yes, they are brilliant marketers. The marketers set the prices, remember??

You can carve out a niche for yourself. Once you discover your unique gifts, your God-given talents, you can become a specialist. You can market in such a way that folks will wait in line for you to do what it is you do so well. When you are on purpose, you can name your price. It takes savvy marketing to make sure everyone knows about you and how helpful you can be.

Good financial data, solid marketing efforts. You are unstoppable.

Man, I think this is so much fun. To do what you love and make lots of money.

STEP #7

Just do it.

"OFF TO WORK!"

With just a bit of trepidation, Sally embarks on her home-based business. She figures if it doesn't work out, she can always go back to work at the car dealership. As long as she keeps track of the numbers, she will always know if she's winning or losing the business game.

If the actual numbers don't make her dreams come true, don't help her fulfill her purpose, she can change...her prices, how she operates, how she organizes her time...or she can quit. It would not be the worst thing if Wall O'Wonders didn't work out. She wouldn't die. The 'goal police' wouldn't come and take her away. She would be fine.

Deepak Chopra calls this the law of detachment. Create the dream, work the plan, and don't worry about the outcome. It's amazing how courageous you become when you let go of your attachment to the outcome.

Just keep an eye on the numbers, the money. That way you'll know how you are doing, statistically.

Sally is blessed to have the emotional support of Big Dog and the kids, and especially fortunate to have Joey as a mentor.

Sally is busy right out of the gate with Wall O' Wonders. She must market and sell her services. She has to handle the phone. (Mike, her son, was discovered answering the business line with a hearty, "Hey Yo!"). She needs to order supplies and paint. She visits with customers and puts together bids. She hears the word, "No." But, to her amazement, she is getting jobs, at her prices.

Each day Sally clicks the sales and expense figures into her computer accounting program. She is amazed to find she really likes the numbers! She kind of understands the Balance Sheet and the Income Statement. She re-reads *Where Did the Money Go?* and starts running weekly financials just to see how she's doing.

After a couple of months, Joey reminds her that it is time to meet with the accountant. The primary reason for having a good tax accountant??

Don't go to jail.

Keeping you out of jail. That's what your accountant is for.

SHOPPING FOR AN ACCOUNTANT

Thirteen years ago Hot Rod and I went shopping for an accountant. Hot Rod's buddy and partner Richard Yox had just died. Yox had always done the books and filed the tax returns.

Yox took an aggressive approach to the IRS. He was cross-hair-focused on making sure that Uncle Sam didn't get one extra penny from Hot Rod & Yox Plumbing and Heating. They got audited once in 1981. The IRS wrote HR&Y a check for $11. Since then we've never been audited. I'm crossing my fingers and knocking on wood that I don't ever have to go through an audit. I suspect, however, that after dealing with Yox, the auditor stamped "DON'T GO THERE" on our file.

Anyway, after Yox died, Hot Rod and I decided to use a professional tax accountant to do our year-end tax filing. We were doing errands one day when we noticed a new sign going up in a little office plaza. Datasyst accounting services. Only, the "D" was backwards. Hmmmm. That indicated that they were either clever, which is a good thing for an accountant to be, or inaccurate, which is a very bad thing for an accountant to be. We pulled in to pay them a visit.

Brenda Paull looks like Bonnie Raitt. She's got wild, red-moving-to-silver hair. She laughs easily and smiles all the time. Brenda invited us to sit down and chat. She told us her story...

Brenda had worked for the IRS for 10 years. Then she went middle-age crazy. She quit her job, got unmarried and started to do what she wanted to do. She figured a good new career would be helping folks protect themselves from the insane jaws of the IRS. So she started preparing tax returns. She does absolutely bulletproof returns. Bring on the auditors. Hah! She knows their methods. Let 'em try!

Brenda met Steve Paull at a costume party on Halloween at a ski patrol party in Park City, Utah. If you don't know this, ski patrollers are serious about parties. They are up there with Vikings' fans and roofers. They discovered they both followed the Grateful Dead. It was instant love. They moved in together, in a teepee in the mountains, and got married at some point.

Steve was also middle-age crazy. And he had been so for about 20 years. Once upon a time, Steve used to wear a suit and tie and punch into the Silicone Valley computer corporate world every day from 9 to 5. I had a hard time believing this when Steve walked into the office and shook hands with us. He had a permanently attached smile, and a long white ponytail. He loved to say, "For sure."

Steve and Brenda decided to go into business together as Datasyst. Brenda would do the accounting, Steve would funnel all the information into the computers. It was a good idea. As it turned out, we were their first customer! I was pregnant with Max, HR was just recovering from Yox's early departure...we were all dealing with endings and new beginnings. It was an auspicious first meeting with our new accountant.

At this time, I was doing the books by hand in one of those heavy red accounting books. Brenda did the taxes at year end and that was it. This worked pretty well for a couple of years. Then we started to get busy. And HR and I started to starve.

You know my story of meeting Frank Blau. Frank hit me — hard, between the eyes — with the Gospel of Good Business. After that, I met with Steve and Brenda and told them I was going to raise our prices, and computerize our accounting. Brenda said, "Good for you. We'd be glad to help."

Steve said, "For sure!"

Brenda offered to do all the data entry. That could have been a fine way to handle the books. But Frank made me realize that I needed to know the financials inside and out. For me, that meant doing it myself, until I understood it. With a computer and an accounting program, I could generate the financials. Then, I could hand it off once I got it figured out.

I'm lucky that I didn't know how much work it would be to computerize our company. I never would have done it. I didn't realize that I would have to learn double-entry accounting. But Brenda helped. She was patient as I pored over the chart of accounts and figured out how we were going to keep track of everything. If you are not computerized, bite the bullet and do it. Sure, the conversion is hell, but heaven lies on the other side. Accounting and computers are made for each other.

THE *REAL* BOOKS VS. THE *PRETEND* BOOKS.

I got the accounting system installed, but I still had to figure out how much to charge. A new year had begun. I took out the calculator and, using Brenda's nicely assembled tax returns, I figured out how much it had cost us to run the company the past year. I did a break-even analysis of the data and found out how much it cost us, per man, per hour to operate Hot Rod & Yox.

$$\frac{\text{Total costs of direct labor + total indirect costs}}{\text{Total number of billable hours}}$$

I came up with something in the neighborhood of $42 dollars per billable hour for overhead and labor. Then, I realized something very important. So important that I am going to write this in bold print...

That's what the break-even amount was using the real numbers from the previous year. That was the year in which we paid ourselves $30,000 (for the two of us!) and our top technician — a man who can fix anything on the face of this planet — made less than $20,000.

Brenda was in charge of tax compliance. She needed the real numbers, the actual dollars taken in and spent. I needed to figure out how much we were going to charge. If I used the real numbers in my calculations, I was doomed to another pitiful year. Just like last year! I took out a columnar pad and wrote down the pretend numbers. How much did I want to spend on ourselves and our wonderful team? I referred to the real numbers...on every line of the income statement I was scrimping. I beefed up my projected costs. And I created a selling price that would allow the coming year's real numbers to look like my pretend numbers.

To calculate break-even and figure your selling prices, you need to create *pretend* numbers. Do your calculations based on what you *hope* to spend, what you *want* to pay yourself and your valuable employees. Write down pretend numbers. Then determine what you need to charge to make your dreams come true.

We set our selling price for an hour of labor at almost four times what it was the year before. Brenda and Steve were totally supportive. In fact, they raised their prices too! They were indeed clever. We all started to make money.

A lot of accountants don't get this. Your accountant might tell you, "You can't charge that, you'll price yourself out of the market!" or "You'll have to pay a lot of taxes on that kind of income." If so, you might need a new accountant. To make the process easy for you, here is a handy checklist for shopping for a new accountant:

Handy Accountant Shopping Checklist...

If 9 or more of these statements apply to your accountant, you have a winner.

- ▲ His primary business goal is to help you make tons of money.
- ▲ She loves when you raise your prices. It means you will both make more money.
- ▲ He asks, "How can I help you get the kind of information you need to fine-tune this company?"
- ▲ She signs the returns with a 'smiley face' next to your best ever numbers.
- ▲ He offers to go over every line of the financial reports until you are sure you understand them.
- ▲ She understands that taxes are a cost of doing business and insists that your selling price is high enough to cover them.
- ▲ He offers to train your new data entry employees so that they get a clear understanding of the accounting program and basic accounting principles. At his place, on your nickel.
- ▲ She loves the 'sailboat' fund idea and suggests you add $10 to every service call to contribute to the boat purchase.
- ▲ He makes a lot of money himself.
- ▲ She pushes you to start the fully funded profit sharing plan and look into ESOP options.
- ▲ He or she smiles a lot, and has lots of experience confronting the IRS.

ABSOLUTELY SENSATIONAL RESOURCES FOR LEARNING TO SELL VALUE NOT PRICE!

Sally picks up a copy of *Success* magazine at the grocery store one day. She devours it! She is absolutely on fire with new marketing ideas and inspired by stories of people just like her who have created wonderful businesses.

An article in the magazine claims that sales skills are not something you are born with, they are learned. This really gets Sally's attention. She doesn't like having to sell her services. She is uncomfortable quoting prices and asking for the sale. Maybe some sales training would be helpful.

Sally is pretty smart!

Joey has a whole audiotape library of wonderful sales trainers and is happy to loan Sally the programs. How convenient! Sally can listen to tapes while she's driving around doing errands. And she can rehearse her sales skills in the car — practice with pretend customers. At night her bedside table is loaded with self-help books, full of advice from the world's greatest salespeople and business experts.

Here are a few absolute must-have books and audio programs:
- ▲ Tom Hopkins – any tape, any book. His delivery is very laid back and easy to listen to.
- ▲ Zig Ziglar – *See You at the Top*. Zig coined the wonderful sales line, "You can get whatever you want if you help enough people get what they want."
- ▲ Harry Beckwith – *Selling the Invisible*. Marketing basics to help you communicate WHY you are the best in town.
- ▲ Jay Conrad Levinson – *Guerilla Marketing*. Zillions of creative ideas for marketing.
- ▲ Harry Friedman – *No Thanks, I'm Just Looking*. Best book on sales. Period.

Once you figure out how much you're going to charge, you are going to have to become a salesperson and marketer. Too many ignorant folks are out there setting selling prices that have no basis in cost. So you are competing with companies whose prices are a fraction of yours. If you can't communicate why you are better, cleaner, neater, nicer, faster...whatever it is that only you are...you are going to hear a lot of "No"s.

Don't count on your competitors to support you in your efforts to improve the industry. Success can be a lonely road. In fact,

YOU ARE GOING TO NEED SOME NEW FRIENDS.

Maybe the worst part is the loneliness. You decide to make changes at your small shop. You want your life to have meaning, to feel that what you're doing is important. So you redefine your company. Crank up the red carpet customer service. Your selling price allows for a real, professional salary for you, career benefits for your staff, extras to make the risk and headache worthwhile.

If everyone in your industry would stand tall they would all be better off, right? So you start to preach the gospel of good business. At association meetings, you're sharing your philosophies of business to anyone who will listen.

"We deserve to make a living doing what we do. We gotta stick together! Act like professionals and charge accordingly. No more low-ball pricing! We can all move up the ladder together!"

Of course, the chorus chants, "Darn straight! That's what *I've* been saying!" and an intoxicating moment of solidarity compels you to buy a round of drinks. Better days are coming, you promise yourself, as the glasses clink.

Then, on Monday morning, you walk up to the supply house counter and hear the last line of a conversation, "...rip off artist...giving the rest of us a bad name." You don't think much of it until you lose a sale, by over $200, to one of your competitors. This is the same fellow who was whining about how hard it is to make a buck with all those *other guys* and their cut-throat pricing.

Face it, my friend. If you plan to make a success of yourself and your business, you will probably stand alone in your marketplace. Because your success will annoy all the other folks who have given up! They have gotten comfortable with the idea that 'it can't be done here, not in our town.' So when you start making changes, well, one of two things could happen with your competitors:

1. They realize that they have been *wrong.*

2. They decide that *you* are wrong.

The first option involves fundamental change, hard work and criticism. The second involves no work at all...just more of the same, peppered with sarcastic snips at you while waiting for parts at the supply house.

You see, as nice as it would be for the whole industry to start flying straight, it ain't going to happen. Chances are you will stand alone if you choose to act like, and charge like, a professional. And some days the loneliness can make you want to pack it in.

Would it help to have a pep talk from someone who has been through tough times and achieved incredible success? Let me introduce you to some of my friends...Jim Rohn, Mark Victor Hansen, Jack Canfield, Steven Covey. I've grown close to these folks and many others through audiotapes! I am addicted to self-help tapes. The speakers' voices have rescued me when I have been sinking in doubt and discouragement. When I hop in my car I always make sure I have a stash of tape programs. On quiet days in the office, I listen to tapes while I work. I have learned more through self-help programs than I ever learned via formal education.

Here are a few of my favorite counselors/teachers/friends. (I've listed the number for phone orders for each one. Also, check out the Amazon website at www.amazon.com. It's a virtual bookstore on the Internet. Search by author and you can order and ship with one 'click' once you set up your account.)

Jim Rohn

My good friend Paul Swan sent me *Challenge to Succeed in the 90's,* one of Jim Rohn's seminars on tape. Wow! What a good story Jim tells of his own road to success! Jim was broke and embarrassed by age 27. Married with kids and only pennies in his pockets, he was introduced to a successful businessman, who became his mentor. This fellow asked Jim why he was not yet successful. When Jim started to blame his dead-end job and the economy for his woes, his mentor stopped him short. "Mr. Rohn," he said, "the problem is you." Jim paid attention to the meat-and-potatoes suggestions for success and shares them in his programs. Here's a sample of Jim Rohn's wisdom...

> *"Success is neither magical or mysterious. Success is the natural consequence of consistently applying basic fundamentals."*

> *"The best motivation is self-motivation. The guy says, 'I wish someone would come by and turn me on.' What if they don't show up? You've got to have a better plan for your life."*

> *"Don't wish it were easier; wish you were better. Don't wish for less problems; wish for more skills. Don't wish for less challenges; wish for more wisdom."*

I love this guy! I had the incredible opportunity to meet him and hear him speak live at the Ohio PHCC convention in 1997. It was Paul Swan's goal to meet Jim Rohn and he arranged to have him speak at the convention. A testimony to the power of goals and planning. To order Jim Rohn's tapes call 1.800.929.0434.

Mark Victor Hansen

Have you heard any of the *Chicken Soup for the Soul* stories on tape? Mark Victor Hansen co-authors the series with Jack Canfield. Listen to a few of these heartwarming stories and see, as Mark says, if it doesn't break up your 'pity party'. Aside from the Chicken Soup stories, Mark has an incredible library of self-help books on tape. His riches-to-rags-to riches story is inspiring...following his heart and his mentor R. Buckminster Fuller, Mark was building geodesic domes in the 1970's. When the oil embargo hit, his plastic-dependent company sank and Mark lost $2 million in one day. He recovered with the help of an audiotape called *Are You the Cause or Are You the Effect?* by Cavett Robert. Mark listened to the tape 237 *times,* bearing witness to the power of repetition! He started over...and became an expert in sales and sales training. Mark targeted the insurance and chiropractic industries. Here are a few quotes from Mark...

> *"Even in the worst depression, 25% of businesses are booming — in your industry find out what they're doing and do it."*

> *"Real leaders like Lee Iacocca see vast possibilities and sell their dreams to their companies, their employees, their funding sources, their government and their buying public."*

> *"The true world of causation lies within your mind. What you experience in life, whether prosperity or poverty, is the effect of your thoughts. Change your thinking, and you automatically change your results."*

73

Mark believes in having BIG dreams. Forget realistic. Landing on the moon was never a realistic goal! His delivery and enthusiasm are catching. Mark is my first listening choice when I need a shot-in-the-arm.

Mark and his co-author **Jack Canfield** wrote my favorite self-help book of all time: *The Aladdin Factor: How to Ask For and Get Everything You Want.* This book outlines how to ask...for sales, wealth, attention...so that you get it. Nice! Mark and Jack know the power of the parable. Stories are what you remember, what makes the lesson 'stick'. Call 1.800.929.0439 to order *Chicken Soup for the Soul* and the rest of Mark Victor Hansen's library on tape.

Stephen Covey

No one is better than Stephen Covey for helping you discover what is really important in your life. His most famous audio book is *The Seven Habits of Highly Effective People.* But my favorite program is called *First Things First.* Stephen suggests that more important than climbing the ladder of success is making sure it's resting on the right wall. What if you climb to the top...and don't like where you end up? His guidelines for prioritizing and planning are the best! Stephen Covey's materials can be ordered from 1.800.654.1776. A couple of his thoughts...

> *"To leverage our time, we should devote less attention to activities that are urgent but unimportant and more time to those things that are important but not necessarily urgent."*

> *"Win-win is the attitude of seeking mutual benefit and it begins with a commitment to explore all options until a mutually satisfactory solution is reached, or to make no deal at all."*

The *best* part is that these friends are introducing me to their friends. Jim Rohn turned me on to George S. Clason, who wrote *The Richest Man in Babylon* — a simple financial plan that will handle debt and insure personal wealth. Mark Victor Hansen suggested I meet Napoleon Hill and learn how to *Think and Grow Rich.* May I also recommend L. Ron Hubbard's tape *The Affinity-Reality-Communication Triangle.* It's a perfect explanation of the mechanics behind communication and understanding. And Barbara Sher has a wonderful methodology for getting things *done* in her audio book *Wishcraft.* I could go on and on...

These great teachers are available anytime and anywhere. Make your drive time class time. Learn from their experiences. Try their techniques and methods. Once upon a time you went to school. Now it's time to learn.

And as you develop yourself and your company, I promise you this: you will attract new friends who delight in your success. You can share your goals and dreams with them and help each other grow and prosper. There is a natural gravitational pull between like minds.

As for those who would rather criticize and belittle you...

> *"Never retreat. Never explain. Get it done and let them howl."*
>
> BENJAMIN JOWETT

74

STEP #8

Check the statistics.

Take responsibility for the score. Make changes. Try again.

"HOW DID I DO??"

Sally and Joey have met at least once a month since Sally started Wall O' Wonders. Today, Sally is proud to show Joey her Balance Sheet and Income Statement for her first whole year of business. Here's a recap of year one's statistics....

- ▲ By keeping track of the hours that she billed to the customers, Sally knows she generated 912 actual billable hours. Note on the Income Statement the Sales - Painting Labor. 912 x $144 = $131,328.

- ▲ The corresponding Direct Cost - Painting Labor is $27,360. Wall O'Waters paid Sally $30 per hour to generate the 912 billable hours.

- ▲ The payroll taxes were paid. See the amounts in Costs - Sally's Painting PR tax and Sally's Owner's PR tax.

- ▲ Sally received the perks and retirement contributions. Isn't that nice? I bet she never would have paid those dollars without a budget.

- ▲ The perks and retirement amounts will have tax consequences, but she will meet with her accountant next week to discuss and plan her tax strategies.

- ▲ Note there is no actual Replacement cost expense. She priced for it, but didn't use the dollars yet.

- ▲ In some cases Sally spent less than she budgeted, in most she spent more.

- ▲ Sales were pretty darn close to the budgeted figures.

Take a moment to look at Sally's projected sales and expenses to the actual sales and expenses.

"Well, Joey, how did I do?"

WALL O' WONDERS
4321 Wander Lane
Hometown, USA

ACTUAL VS. BUDGETED
PROFIT & LOSS STATEMENT
DECEMBER 31, YEAR 1

	Actual	% of Sales	Budgeted	% of Sales	$ Difference
Sales Income					
Sales - Painting Labor	$131,328.00	89.0%	$144,000.00	89.5%	($12,672.00)
Sales - Painting Materials	$16,218.75	11.0%	$16,875.00	10.5%	($656.25)
Total Sales Income	$147,546.75	100.0%	$160,875.00	100.0%	($13,328.25)
Direct Costs					
Costs - Sally's Painting Labor	$27,360.00	18.5%	$30,000.00	18.7%	($2,640.00)
Costs - Sally's Painting PR Tx	$7,114.00	4.8%	$8,000.00	4.9%	($886.00)
Costs - Painting Materials	$12,875.00	8.7%	$13,500.00	8.4%	($625.00)
Total Direct Costs	$47,349.00	32.0%	$51,500.00	32.0%	($4,151.00)
Gross Profit	$100,197.75	67.9%	$109,375.00	68.0%	($9,177.25)
Indirect Costs					
Sally's Owner's Salary	$30,000.00	20.3%	$30,000.00	18.6%	$0.00
Sally's Owner's PR Taxes	$8,000.00	5.4%	$8,000.00	4.9%	$0.00
Sally's Perks	$8,000.00	5.4%	$8,000.00	4.9%	$0.00
Sally's Retirement Contribution	$12,000.00	8.1%	$12,000.00	7.5%	$0.00
Accounting Expense	$3,200.00	2.2%	$1,570.00	1.0%	$1,630.00
Advertising	$2,250.45	1.5%	$1,530.00	1.0%	$720.45
Bad Debt	352.00	0.2%	$600.00	0.3%	($248.00)
Equipment - Depreciation	$500.00	0.3%	$500.00	0.3%	$0.00
Equipment - Replacement	$0.00	0.2%	$1,395.00	0.8%	($1,395.00)
Dues	$600.00	0.4%	$600.00	0.3%	$0.00
Entertainment	$1,545.67	1.1%	$600.00	0.3%	$945.67
Insurance	$2,355.60	1.6%	$1,695.00	1.0%	$660.60
Interest	$466.56	0.3%	$450.00	0.3%	$16.56
Lease - Van	$2,520.00	1.7%	$2,520.00	1.6%	$0.00
Licenses	$75.00.	0.0%	$75.00	0.0%	$0.00
Maintenance	$849.01	0.6%	$360.00	0.2%	$489.01
Office Supplies	$1,278.99	0.8%	$1,055.00	0.7%	$223.99
Postage	$232.00	0.1%	$190.00	0.1%	$42.00
Rent & Utilities	$2,580.00	1.7%	$2,580.00	1.6%	$0.00
Repairs	$329.74	0.2%	$500.00	0.3%	($170.26)
Shop Supplies	$977.65	0.7%	$1,020.00	0.6%	($42.35)
Telephone	$1,233.45	0.8%	$840.00	0.5%	$393.45
Travel	$1,355.92	0.9%	$790.00	0.5%	$565.92
Uniforms	$789.10	0.5%	$130.00	0.1%	$659.10
Total Indirect Costs	$81,491.14	55.2%	$77,000.00	47.9%	$4,491.14
Operating Profit	$18,706.61	12.7%	$32,375.00	20.1%	($13,668.39)
Other Income					
Other Expenses					
Net Profit / (Loss)	$18,706.61	12.7%	$32,375.00	20.1%	($13,668.39)

WALL O' WONDERS
4321 Wander Lane
Hometown, USA

ACTUAL BALANCE SHEET
DECEMBER 31, YEAR 1

Assets
  Current Assets
    Checking Account $9,197.17
  Total Current Assets $11,756.00
  Fixed Assets $20,953.17
  Equipment
    Computer - Original Cost $1,975.00
    Computer - Accum Depreciation ($395.00)
    Airbrush - Original Cost $525.00
    Airbrush - Accum Depreciation ($105.00)
  Total Equipment - $2,000.00
  Total Fixed Assets $2,000.00
Total Assets $22,953.17

Liabilities
  Current Liabilities
    Business Credit Card $2,246.56
  Total Current Liabilities $2,246.56
Total Liabilities $2,246.56

Equity
  Owner's Equity
    Owner's Investment $2,000.00
  Total Owner's Equity $2,000.00
  Current Year Earnings $18,706.61
Total Equity $20,706.61

Total Liability & Equity $22,953.17

"Sally, I am really proud of you. You thought no one would pay your prices and now you are booked up three weeks in advance. Well done.

"Let's go over the numbers and make a game plan for year number two.

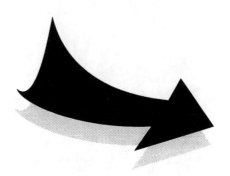

You still need to beef up your retirement and insurance amounts. Sally, you are over 40 now. You don't have too many years left to create your retirement nest egg. Better beef it up.

"And if anything happened to you, the rest of your family would be in dire financial straits. You must add disability insurance this year. Last year I didn't press you because I knew how nervous you were about your selling price. Now that you are doing so well, you can budget in more cost and raise your prices accordingly. We need to boost that bottom line a bit, too."

"I can't believe I was going to charge $30 an hour," Sally says. "Just for grins, I ran an Income Statement that replaced the Sales - Painting Labor with 912 hours at $30 per hour. Check it out! A bottom line of *negative* $85, 261.39.

Wall O' Wonders

4321 Wander Lane
Hometown, USA

Profit & Loss Statement
WHAT WOULD HAVE HAPPENED AT $30/HOUR!

Sales Income			% of Sales
Sales - Painting Labor	$27,360.00		62.8%
Sales - Painting Materials	$16,218.75		37.2%
Total Sales Income		$43,578.75	100.0%
Direct Costs			
Costs - Sally's Painting Labor	$27,360.00		62.8%
Costs - Sally's Painting PR Tx	$7,114.00		16.3%
Costs - Painting Materials	$12,875.00		29.5%
Total Direct Costs		$47,349.00	108.6%
Gross Profit		($3,770.25)	<8.6%>
Indirect Costs			
Sally's Owner's Salary	$30,000.00		68.8%
Sally's Owner's PR Taxes	$8,000.00		18.4%
Sally's Perks	$8,000.00		18.4%
Sally's Retirement Contribution	$12,000.00		27.5%
Accounting Expense	$3,200.00		7.3%
Advertising	$2,250.45		5.2%
Bad Debt	$352.00		0.8%
Equipment - Depreciation	$500.00		1.2%
Dues	$600.00		1.4%
Entertainment	$1,545.67		3.6%
Insurance	$2,355.60		5.4%
Interest	$466.56		1.0%
Lease - Van	$2,520.00		5.8%
Licenses	$75.00		0.2%
Maintenance	$849.01		1.9%
Office Supplies	$1,278.99		2.9%
Postage	$232.00		0.5%
Rent & Utilities	$2,580.00		5.9%
Repairs	$329.74		0.8%
Shop Supplies	$977.65		2.2%
Telephone	$1,233.45		2.8%
Travel	$1,355.92		3.1%
Uniforms	$789.10		1.8%
Total Indirect Costs		$81,491.14	187.0%
Operating Profit		($85,261.39)	<195.6%>
Other Income			
Other Expenses			
Net Profit / (Loss)		($85,261.39)	<195.6%>

"Then I ran the same report again, but took out all my pay, perks and retirement. Because I *wouldn't* have paid myself with those numbers. This is what my Income Statement would have looked like if I didn't listen to you, Joey. Pretty meager. Total Sales of $43,578.75. Nothing for me. Just over $7,000 for the company.

WALL O' WONDERS
4321 Wander Lane
Hometown, USA

PROFIT & LOSS STATEMENT
AT $30/HOUR — I WOULDN'T HAVE PAID ME!

			% of Sales
Sales Income			
Sales - Painting Labor	$27,360.00		62.8%
Sales - Painting Materials	$16,218.75		37.2%
Total Sales Income		$43,578.75	100.0%
Direct Costs			
Costs - Painting Materials	$12,875.00		29.5%
Total Direct Costs		$12,875.00	29.5%
Gross Profit		$30,703.75	70.5%
Indirect Costs			
Accounting Expense	$3,200.00		7.3%
Advertising	$2,250.45		5.2%
Bad Debt	$352.00		0.8%
Equipment - Depreciation	$500.00		1.2%
Dues	$600.00		1.4%
Entertainment	$1,545.67		3.6%
Insurance	$2,355.60		5.4%
Interest	$466.56		1.0%
Lease - Van	$2,520.00		5.8%
Licenses	$75.00		0.2%
Maintenance	$849.01		1.9%
Office Supplies	$1,278.99		2.9%
Postage	$232.00		0.5%
Rent & Utilities	$2,580.00		5.9%
Repairs	$329.74		0.8%
Shop Supplies	$977.65		2.2%
Telephone	$1,233.45		2.8%
Travel	$1,355.92		3.1%
Uniforms	$789.10		1.8%
Total Indirect Costs		$23,491.14	53.9%
Operating Profit		$7,212.61	16.6%
Other Income			
Other Expenses			
Net Profit / (Loss)		$7,212.611	16.6%

"I feel like a real winner, Joey. Thanks. And there's more. Not all the data I want is available from the Income Statement and Balance Sheet. I put together this little monthly summary report. It helps me keep an eye on the important ratios...gross margin and profit margin. And I keep a running tally of billable hours. Also, I check my break-even per billable hour every month to make sure that my selling price is accurate. Pretty cool, huh?

"One thing is clear. As a one person shop I am not going to be able to grow my company without adding people, or products or both. Maybe I should play with the budgets a bit...plug in another painter, maybe add wallpaper to our product line. What do you think, Joey?"

"Sally, I think you're doing fine!" Joey said with a smile.

WALL O' WONDERS
Monthly Summary of Critical Numbers   Month:_____19____   By:_____

	MONTH				YTD			LAST YEAR 100%
SALES		_____ 100%		SALES		_____ 100%		
DIRECT COSTS				DIRECT COSTS				
Materials/Other_____+				Materials/Other_____+				
Labor _____=		_____ _____%		Labor _____=		_____ _____%		_____%
GROSS MARGIN/GROSS PROFIT		_____ _____%		GROSS MARGIN/GROSS PROFIT		_____ _____%		_____%
OVERHEAD		_____ _____%		OVERHEAD		_____ _____%		_____%
NET PROFIT		_____ _____%		NET PROFIT		_____ _____%		_____%
OWNER'S SALARY - Paid		_____		OWNER'S SALARY - Paid		_____		
# OF BILLABLE HRS/MONTH		_____		# OF BILLABLE HRS/MONTH		_____		
BREAK-EVEN per BILLABLE HOUR				BREAK-EVEN per BILLABLE HOUR				
Overhead _____ + Direct Costs _____				Overhead _____ + Direct Costs _____				
/Billable Hours _____ =		_____		/Billable Hours _____ =		_____		

How else can you expand YOU?

You see that the biggest challenge with selling your unique service is that you are bound by the number of billable hours that you can create. An hour of your time should always have a hefty price tag. You are that valuable.

How can Sally, and you, expand your companies? How can you duplicate your services without resorting to cloning?

Bring on the associates.

What if you could share your knowledge with others and create new providers of your services? I know no one can do what you do *exactly* like you do it. But could they do it well enough for customers to want it? Could you find someone who does what you do even better than you? Or just different enough that a whole new set of customers opens up?

You see, what happens if you get sick? Or you might just grow sick of doing the work you do, day in and day out. Operating as a one-person company is a delightful, necessary way to start your company. But it is a hard model to maintain. Consider growing your company, teaching people how to do what you do so that you don't always have to do it.

There is a terrific, must-read book that explains the process of growing a company. Wouldn't it be nice if your company wasn't dependent on you every second of every day? What about adding employees or associates to help you provide your purposeful services?

- ▲ You can add people to provide more billable hours.
- ▲ You can add people to do some of the administrative functions, and that would free you up to provide more billable hours.

Your company is either shrinking or growing. Nothing in this universe stays the same. By bringing more people into your organization, you can reach even more customers, spread around even more of your beneficial services.

As a one-person company, you might think growing into a corporate giant is beyond you in this lifetime. Sally is thinking, "Hey, I'm 40 years old already! I'm out of time." Remember, you can get whatever you want. If you want to be a corporate giant, then, by all means, do it. Mary Kay Ash of Mary Kay Cosmetics — you know, the pink Cadillac lady — didn't start her multi-billion dollar company until she was 45 years old.

You can light the way, and share your purpose, your vision. Not everyone wants to be a leader. It might be someone else's purpose to support your purpose. If who you are and what you do is compelling enough, you will attract people to share your vision.

Crunch the numbers. Find out what your break-even cost would be if you added staff. Create a selling price that will support your growth. Don't scrimp on employee benefits. Your company should provide careers not just jobs. How can you develop your pay structure so that those who produce the best numbers make the most money? Can you share the numbers with them? Can you play a straight game with all your employees?

(The next book in the MAXROHR Business Basics Series is called, *Help Me Find Some Help!* It's a bare bones essential manual on finding and hiring life-long employees. It uses the same track-the-numbers approach that you've learned in this book and in *Where Did the Money Go?* Learn the basics and become a great boss! Call toll-free 1.877.MAXROHR [1.877.629.7647] for availability and order information, or you can order online at www.maxrohr.com).

SELL MORE PRODUCTS.

Notice that when Sally added paint sales to her financial picture, net profit went up! Cool, huh? As an artist, Sally can supply the paint and use the material sale to generate more net profit. Remember, all costs generate profit dollars. When you create a profit margin on your costs, the higher the costs the higher the profits.

But when Sally sells paint, her customers expect her to lay it on the walls. So her material sales generate billable hours, and she only has a finite number of billable hours. Therefore, there is a limit to the number of gallons of paint she can sell — that limit is the number of billable hours it will take to put it on the walls.

Are you with me? If someone wanted to buy some paint only, and NOT have Sally work her magic with it to create a Wall O'Wonder, they wouldn't buy that paint from Sally. Sally is not the best value when someone wants to make a paint only purchase. She couldn't possibly compete with Home Depot and Sears when it comes to selling material only.

That's why Home Depot and Sears are NO THREAT to the small shop that is providing unique services! You sell a service, they sell commodities and products. There is room for all of you in the marketplace.

But what kind of products could you sell that would add profit dollars to your bottom line? Products that don't require billable hours.

- ▲ Exclusive product lines. For instance, Sally might look for a complimentary fabric line that matches her wall designs. Fabrics that are available only through designers, not through Home Depot or other home center stores.
- ▲ Sally could take pictures of her murals and sell the photos as posters, or a calendar, coffee mugs, greeting cards...etc.
- ▲ Sally could convert her murals to vinyl stickers that peel-n-stick right to the wall.

What could you do to duplicate your work? Can you convert your skill to a product? Get creative — this can be a very liberating and profitable avenue!

SELL INFORMATION!

Could you sell your knowledge? Could you put your experience and expertise into audio or videotape form and teach others what you know? Could you write a book?

Sally could teach others to do wall murals and 'faux' finishing. She could produce information products that teach professionals these sophisticated techniques. She could even share information on how to run a successful specialty painting business, once she gets some experience under her belt.

She could teach do-it-yourself-ers how to create walls of wonder. No, their work wouldn't look like hers. She could provide her services for those who really want her work and are willing to pay for it. But with Sally's painting techniques, a do-it-yourself-er might create an awesome mural!

Could you share your knowledge? How can you package your information? How can you better serve your purpose by making more of your skills and knowledge available?

Whatever you decide, write down the pretend numbers. Make your best guess on the numbers you don't know. Do a budget. Then, meticulously track your real numbers every single day! The key to your success is in the financial statements. Look at them! Assess your performance. Adjust as you need to and PRESS ON!

HELPFUL HINT

Fill in the monthly summary of critical numbers sheet every month (see page 81). Watch these critical numbers. Overall, percentages are a better gauge than dollar amounts. As you fine tune your company, over time, you'll see that percentages don't vary as much as dollars.

PROVE ME WRONG!!!

Dear Reader,

You made it this far. Congratulations for all you've learned. But I wonder...

Do you think that this pricing system could ever work for you? Do you think that you could charge the going rate and make a living doing what you love?

Would you like to prove me wrong?

Please do. Just document everything you do in financial statements. You could teach me something.

You see, I have a theory. My theory is that if you were to confront the real numbers every month, every week, every day, you would make your company successful, or you would call it quits. It doesn't matter what you try as long as you keep score.

This method of pricing is based on standard accounting. It's nothing magical. There is more than one way to skin a cat. By reading the financial reports we can get pretty great data. We can know with certainty if the cat got skinned. Or not.

Reach me personally with any questions, comments or friendly conversation. My mission is to you make a living doing what you love. So call me and let me know how I can help.

Love, peace and prosperity,

Ellen Rohr   XOXOXOXOXO

I bet you learned a lot...take this test and see for yourself!

Take this quiz...let's see what you learned.

1.   Your selling price should NOT be based on:
( ) Your costs of doing business.
( ) How much money you want to make.
( ) How much money you want to spend.
( ) What the market will bear.

2.   What is the basic accounting formula?
( ) Sales - Profits = Loss
( ) Assets = Liabilities + Owners' Equity
( ) A little bit of wish plus a pinch of luck = who knows what

3.   What is the difference between *margin* and *markup*?

_____
_____
_____

4.   If you provide a service that costs you $100 to produce, and you want to make a 20% profit on the sale of that service, how much should you charge? Show your work.

_____
_____
_____

5.   What does *break-even* mean?
( ) You will even break his arm if your customer refuses to pay for your services.
( ) The total cost of creating your products and services.
( ) The selling price of your services.
( ) The slope of a golf green.

6.   You are not allowed to create a budget that includes items like *vacations* and *college funds* as these items are not officially tax-deductible according to the IRS. True or False? Explain....

_____
_____
_____

7.   Today's accounting programs are so good and easy to use, you don't need an accountant anymore! True or False?

8. Who pays for your advertising?
    ( ) you do.
    ( ) your mother, thank goodness.
    ( ) your business partner, the one with the inherited fortune!
    ( ) your customer.

9. As a service provider it is much more professional to send a bill, than to present an invoice at the time the work is done. True or False?

10. To go out of business is a sign of weakness, even if the business is losing money. The successful business people never quit. True or False?

Here are the answers...how did you do?

1. Your selling price should NOT be based on:
    ( ) Your costs of doing business.
    ( ) How much money you want to make.
    ( ) How much money you want to spend.
    (x) What the market will bear.

    Your selling price should be based on your costs of doing business, how much you want to make and how much you want to spend. You might look at the going rate in your market to see if you are up to the challenge of selling your prices in that market. Ask if *you can bear the market*, not what will the market bear.   And then proceed courageously to charge whatever you need to for your dreams to come true.

2. What is the basic accounting formula?
    ( ) Sales - Profits = Loss
    (x) Assets = Liabilities + Owners' Equity
    ( ) A little bit of wish plus a pinch of luck = who knows what

    If you need a hand understanding basic accounting terms and the Balance Sheet and the Income Statement, go back to *Where Did the Money Go?*. Call me at 1.877.MAXROHR (1.877.629.7647) to order, or visit www.maxrohr.com.   It will help you learn the basics that this book builds on.

3. What is the difference between *margin* and *markup?*

    Markup is a method of increasing costs to create a selling price by multiplying the costs by a percentage. The profit margin is the percent difference between break-even and the selling price. See page 50.

4. If you provide a service that costs you $100 to produce, and you want to make a 20% profit on the sale of that service, how much should you charge? Show your work.

    $$\frac{\_\_\_\_\_\ \$100\ \_\_\_\_\_}{.80} = \$125$$

    Refer back to the forms on page 53 to review the formula for creating a selling price.

5.   What does *break-even* mean?
       ( ) You will even break his arm if your customer refuses to pay for your services.
       (x) The total cost of creating your products and services.
       ( ) The selling price of your services.
       ( ) The slope of a golf green.

If you sell your products and services at break-even, you just cover your costs but you don't make any profit. If you sell for less than break-even you lose money. If you sell for more than break-even, you make a profit. See page 45.

6.   You are not allowed to create a budget that includes items like *vacations* and *college funds* as these items are not officially tax-deductible according to the IRS. True or False? Explain....

False. The budget is just pretend. You don't need to comply with any IRS rules as you set your selling prices. You will compare your actual numbers with your budgeted numbers, however, so it is a good idea to work with your tax accountant as you prepare your budget. But if you really want a boat, create a selling price that is based on numbers that include a boat payment or purchase. It's your dream. Why not? Refer to pages 28-30.

7.   Today's accounting programs are so good and easy to use, you don't need an accountant anymore! True or False?

False! You still need an accountant, especially for his or her expertise with tax laws and requirements. You can create daily financial reports that tell you how your company is doing. Great! But it is a good idea to have your accountant check your figures once a month - at least until you get very good at doing your own accounting. You might find you would rather not become an accounting expert. Fine. But you still need to know how to read and act off of the financial reports. Otherwise, how will you know if what you're doing is making money or not?

8.   Who pays for your advertising?
       ( ) you do.
       ( ) your mother, thank goodness.
       ( ) your business partner, the one with the inherited fortune!
       (x) your customer.

Your customer pays for everything. Every cost is passed on to the customer. The selling price must cover all costs, including generous compensation for you and your employees, and a profit that will allow the company to grow and expand. You are not required to give your customer the lowest price. To prosper, you must offer your customer incredible VALUE for the money he spends with you.

9.   As a service provider it is much more professional to send a bill, than to present an invoice at the time the work is done. True or False?

False. You will do yourself and your customer a favor by adopting a COD policy. Price the job before you provide service. Collect on the spot. Folks expect to pay right away. The only businesses that send a bill are those who are uncertain what they are going to charge. That's not you. See page 57.

10.   To go out of business is a sign of weakness, even if the business is losing money. The successful business people never quit. True or False?

False. Businesses come and go. Personal mission is never abandoned.

Closing Thoughts...

I wrote this article for the December 1998 issue of *The Wethead Gazette*, an on-line newsletter found at www.holohan.com.

Why I love money.

December is here. Already. I have just gotten used to dating my checks with 1998. How did the whole year slip by in just a few moments?

It's possible to alter time. I just haven't figured it out yet. I know it is possible to stretch a moment of my time, to open it, create something in that expanded moment, then snap it shut again. To the rest of the world a second has passed. To me, I have had a long stretch of focused productivity...and emerged with a life-changing book, a revised social security system, a way to eliminate the IRS, a formula for world peace.

I don't know how to do that yet. But I am working on it.

In the meantime, December hits me right between the eyes. How can it be here already? I haven't done all I wanted to do this year. I am behind.

> *"Anything is possible. I've found that it just takes a little longer and costs a little more than I thought it would."*
>
> AL LEVI

Pretend that today is your last day in this lifetime. That's it. Game is up at midnight tonight. What would you really like to do before the clock runs out?

Who would you like to spend your last hours with? Any loose ends that need wrapping up? Any apologies to make? Anyone to forgive? Any prayers to say?

How would you spend your money? Remember, you can't take it with you.

The answers to these questions will give you the keys to making next year your best ever. Because chances are good that you won't die tonight by midnight. You might. But you will probably live through the night, and tomorrow and through all of next year.

The trick is to live as if today were your last day, but plan as if you will never die. In some cultures, the Japanese for instance, people make 50, 100 and 500 year plans. Not because they will live that long. But because they understand that they are merely a piece of the greater whole. They realize one's actions affect everyone.

Your every move impacts all of mankind. Your actions are pro-survival, or contra-survival. You're either helping, or not. There are no neutral actions.

The universe is based on a binary number system. Yes or no. No gray area in the universe.

That's what I love about numbers, about money. Numbers and dollars are pretty objective measurements. Were you profitable, or not? Did you contribute to your family's college fund, insurance benefits, retirement...or not? Did you contribute to the causes that you believe in? You spent lots of money last year...did it help mankind? Did it hinder? What does your checkbook say about you? Money holds us accountable.

That's why I love money. Money talks.

> *"Money is the cause of good things to a good man, and of evil things to a bad man."*
> - Philo

Money isn't everything. It's just an indicator, a gauge, that measures what's important to you. There are other measurements. Like, how many times did you make someone smile? How many times did you laugh? Did you lend a hand and help someone up? Did you pause at something beautiful and give thanks for its existence? Did you hold doors open? Did you say 'please' and 'thank you'? How many times did you offer help? Did you confront evil? Did you fix something that was broken? Turn the other cheek? Stand up for what is right? What did you create? What did you learn? What books did you read? What knowledge did you share?

Did you help? Or hinder. Every action can be measured, surely, and hash-marked as doing one or the other.

I love money. Money is easy. The other yardsticks are more difficult to read.

As you reflect on your life at this moment in time, you may find that you are on the right road. Maybe you are not as far along as you would like to be. But when you are on the right path, it's a fine thing. Good for you.

Perhaps your life looks *nothing* like what you want it to look like. If you don't like your job, your family or where you live, well, you are on the wrong road. And you are going to have to change your operating system. Find a new plan. Switch tracks.

You can always change. You can get better.

How am I doing? Well, on some yardsticks, pretty good. Money, blessedly, is easy to measure. In other areas...Hmmmm. I wish I could expand time.

Thank God for another year.

xoxoxox Ellen

GLOSSARY

ACCOUNTING EQUATION: The balance sheet is based on the basic accounting equation. That is:
Assets = Equities
Equity of the company can be held by someone other than the owner. That is called a liability. Because we always have some liabilities, the accounting equation is usually written...
Assets = Liabilities + Owner's Equity

ACCOUNTS: Business activities cause increases and decreases in your assets, liabilities and equity. Your accounting system records these activities in *accounts*. A number of accounts are needed to summarize the increases and decreases in each asset, liability and owner's equity account on the balance sheet and of each revenue and expense that appears on the income statement. You can have a few accounts or hundreds, depending on the kind of detailed information you need to run your business.

ACCOUNTS PAYABLE: Also called **A/P.** These are bills that your business owes to the government or your suppliers. If you have bought it, but haven't paid for it yet (like when you buy on account) you create an account payable. These are found in the liability section of the balance sheet.

ACCOUNTS RECEIVABLE: Also called **A/R.** When you sell something to someone, and they don't pay you that minute, you create an account receivable. This is the amount of money your customers owe you for products and services that they bought from you...but haven't paid for yet. Accounts receivable are found in the current assets section of the balance sheet.

ACCRUAL BASIS ACCOUNTING: With accrual basis accounting, you 'account for' expenses and sales at the time the transaction occurs. This is the most accurate way of accounting for your business activities. If you sell something to Mrs. Fernwicky today, you would record the sale as of today, even if she plans on paying you in two months. If you buy some paint today, you account for it today, even if you will pay for it next month when the supply house statement comes. **Cash basis accounting** records the sale when the cash is received and the expense when the check goes out. Not as accurate a picture of what is happening at your company.

ASSETS: The stuff the company owns. Anything of value - cash, accounts receivable, trucks, inventory, land. **Current assets** are those that could be converted into cash easily. (Officially, within a year's time.) The most current of current assets is cash, of course. Accounts receivable will be converted to cash as soon as the customer pays, hopefully within a month. So, accounts receivable are current assets. So is inventory.

Fixed assets are those things that you wouldn't want to convert into cash for operating money. For instance, you don't want to sell your building to cover the supply house bill. Assets are listed, in order of *liquidity* (how close it is to cash) on the Balance Sheet.

BALANCE SHEET: The balance sheet reflects the financial condition of the company on a specific date. The basic accounting formula is the basis for the balance sheet:

Assets = Liabilities + Owner's Equity

The balance sheet doesn't start over. It is the cumulative score from day one of the business to the time the report is created.

BILLABLE HOUR: The labor hour that is sold as a service to the customer. For instance, a doctor's exam requires the doctor's time. If your service involves your *time*, the billable hour is a very important number. There are only 24 hours in a day and you and your employees can be of service for only so many of those hours every day. How many? You must keep track with timecards...tallied daily, weekly, monthly, yearly.

Doctors, plumbers, painters, housecleaners, lawyers, baby-sitters...are all limited by the number of hours that they have to provide their services. Knowing your billable hours can help make sure that you are charging enough for your services. All the costs of doing business must be recaptured by the sale of your billable hours.

The ratio of billable hours to the total hours available is called **billable hour efficiency**.

CASH FLOW: The movement and timing of money, in and out of the business. In addition to the balance sheet and the income statement, you may want to report the flow of cash through your business. Your company could be profitable but 'cash poor' and unable to pay your bills. Not good!

A **cash flow statement** helps keep you aware of how much cash came and went for any period of time. A **cash flow projection** would be an educated guess at what the cash flow situation will be for the future - you could use this for your budget.

Suppose you want to buy a new truck with cash. But that purchase will empty the bank account and leave you without any cash for payroll! For cash flow reasons, you might choose to buy a truck on payments instead.

CHART OF ACCOUNTS: A complete listing of every account in your accounting system. Every transaction in your business needs to be recorded, so that you can keep track of things. Think of the chart of accounts as the peg board on which you hang the business activities.

CREDIT: A credit is used in Double-Entry accounting to increase a liability or an equity account. A credit will decrease an asset account. For every credit there is a debit. These are the two balancing components of every journal entry. Credits and debits keep the basic accounting equation (Assets = Liabilities + Owner's Equity) in balance as you record business activities.

DEBIT: A debit is used in Double-Entry accounting to increase an asset account. A debit will decrease a liability or an equity account. For every debit there is a credit.

Note the handy debit and credit rules chart at the end of the book.

DEPRECIATION and ACCUMULATED DEPRECIATION: Depreciation means expensing an asset over a period of time. Depreciation is recorded as an expense and shows up on the income statement. The balancing double-entry is recorded in accumulated depreciation, an account that shows the total amount of depreciation you have recorded for an asset. Accumulated depreciation appears on the balance sheet, right below the asset.

For example, let's say you have a truck that you use for deliveries. Tax laws allow you to expense the cost of that truck over the course of a few years. Each month you will make a journal entry that records the depreciation.

	Debit	Credit
Depreciation Expense	$700	
Accumulated Depreciation		$700

And the truck would be listed on the balance sheet like this...

Assets	
Truck	$20,000
Accumulated Depreciation	($700)

So the asset is listed at its original cost. And the accumulated depreciation account right below it tells you how much of the total cost of the asset has been expensed. You see, that asset will reduce in value over time, right? The asset less the accumulated depreciation amount gives you a rough estimate of the value of the vehicle.

This is an accounting technique. It isn't intended to show you the actual re-sale value of the truck! Some assets increase in value over time. Some lose their value or get used up. Like a truck. Depreciation allows you to expense an asset that gets used up over time.

Note that depreciation is a non-cash expense. You don't get a bill in the mail every month saying, "Pay your depreciation!" The idea is that you could take the dollar amount that you are depreciating every month and put it in the bank. When five years are up (typically, you depreciate a truck over five years) you take that money and buy the company a new truck!

Now, consider this...could you replace the truck you have today with one of equal value in five years for the same selling price? In other words, if you bought a brand new truck in 1998 for $25,000, would you expect the new 2003 model truck to sell for $25,000? By then, a similar truck might cost $40,000. Depreciation can help you plan for replacing your truck but it is not the whole story.

Depreciation is a handy method for expensing an asset that loses value when you use it in your business. Office furniture is another asset that gets used up, so you are allowed by tax law to depreciate it.

DIRECT COSTS: Also called **cost of goods sold, cost of sales or job site expenses**. These are expenses that include labor costs and materials. These expenses can be directly tracked to a specific job. If the job didn't happen, the direct costs wouldn't have been incurred. (Compare direct cost with indirect costs to get a better understanding of the term.) Direct costs are found on the Income Statement, right below the income accounts.

Income - Direct Costs = Gross Margin.

DOUBLE-ENTRY ACCOUNTING: An accounting system used to keep track of business activities. Double-entry accounting maintains the balance sheet:

Assets = Liabilities + Owner's Equity. When dollars are recorded in one account, they must be accounted for in another account in such a way that the activity is well documented and the balance sheet stays in balance.

You may not need to be an expert in Double-Entry accounting, but the person who is responsible for creating the financial statements better get pretty good at it. Remember the law of the universe...what goes around, comes around. This is the essence of Double-Entry accounting.

EQUITY: Funds that have been supplied to the company to get the 'stuff'. Equities show ownership of the assets or claims against the assets. If someone other than the owner has claims on the assets, it is called a **liability**.

Total Assets - Total Liabilities = Net Equity

This is another way of stating the basic accounting equation that emphasizes how much of the assets you own. Net equity is also called **net worth**.

EXPENSE: Also called **costs**. Expenses are decreases in equity. These are dollars paid out to suppliers, vendors, Uncle Sam, employees, charities, etc. Remember to pay bills thankfully, because it takes money to make money. Expenses are listed on the income statement. They should be split into two categories, direct costs and indirect costs. The basic equation for the income statement is:

Revenues - Expenses = Profit

(You'll see a profit if there are more revenues than expenses...or a loss, if expenses are more than revenues.) Remember, all costs need to be included in your selling price. The customer pays for everything. In exchange, you give the customer your services. What a deal!

FINANCIAL STATEMENTS: refer to the balance sheet and the income statement. The balance sheet is a report that shows the financial condition of the company. The income statement (also called the profit and loss statement or the 'P&L') is the profit performance summary.

Financial statements can include the supporting documents like cash flow reports, accounts receivable reports, transaction register, or any report that measures the movement of money in your company.

Financial statements are what the bank wants to see before it loans you money. The IRS insists that you share the score with them, and asks for your financial statements every year.

GENERAL LEDGER: Once upon a time, accounting systems were kept in a book that listed the increases and decreases in all the accounts of the company. That book was called the general ledger. Today, you probably have a computerized accounting system. Still, the general ledger is a collection of all balance sheet and income statement accounts...all the assets, liabilities and equity. It is the report that shows ALL the activity in the company. Often this listing is called a detail trial balance on the report menu of your accounting program.

GROSS MARGIN: Also called **gross profit**. This is how much money you have left after you have subtracted the direct costs from the selling price.

Income - Direct Costs = Gross Margin

This is a good number to scrutinize each month, and to track in terms of percentage to total sales over the course of time. The higher the better with gross margin! You need to have enough money left at this point to pay all your indirect costs and still end up with a profit.

INCOME STATEMENT: also called **the Profit and Loss Statement, or P&L, or Statement of Operations**. This is a report that shows the changes in the equity of the company as a result of business operations. It lists the income (or revenues, or sales), subtracts the expenses and shows you the profit (or loss). This report covers a period of time and summarizes the money in and the money out.

The income statement is like a magnifying glass that shows the detail of activities that cause changes in the equity section of the balance sheet.

INDIRECT COST: Also called **overhead or operating expenses**. These expenses are indirectly related to the services you provide to customers. Indirect costs include office salaries, rent, advertising, telephone, utilities...costs to keep a 'roof overhead'. Every cost that is not a direct cost is an indirect cost. Indirect costs do not go away when sales drop off.

INVENTORY: Also called **stock.** These are materials that you purchase with the intent to sell, but you haven't sold them yet. Inventory is found on the balance sheet under assets. It is considered a current asset because you will convert it into cash as soon as you sell it.

JOURNAL: This is the diary of your business. It keeps track of business activities chronologically. Each business activity is recorded as a journal entry. The double-entry will list the debit account and the credit account for each transaction on the day that it occurred. In the reports menu of your accounting system, the journal entries are listed in the **transaction register.**

LIABILITIES: Like equities, these are sources of assets — how you got the 'stuff'. These are claims against assets by someone other than the owner. This is what the company *owes!* Notes payable, taxes payable and loans are liabilities. Liabilities are categorized as current liabilities (need to pay off within a year's time, like payroll taxes) or long term liabilities (payback time is more than a year, like your building mortgage).

MONEY: Also called **moola, scratch, gold, coins, cash, change, chicken feed, jing, green stuff, etc.** Money is the form we use to exchange goods and services for other goods and services. Used to buy things that you need or want. Beats trading for chickens in the global marketplace.

Money in and of itself is neither good or bad. I want you to make lots of it, and do great things with it!

NET INCOME: Also called **net profit, net earnings, current earnings or bottom line**. (No wonder accounting is confusing — look at all those words that mean the same thing!)

After you have subtracted ALL expenses (including taxes) from revenues, you are left with net income. The word net means basic, fundamental. This is a very important item on the income statement because it tells you how much money is left after business operations. Think of net income like the score of a single basketball game in a series. Net income tells you if you won or lost, and by how much, for a given period of time.

By the way, if net income is a negative number, it's called a loss. You want to avoid those. The net income is reflected on the balance sheet in the equity section, under current earnings (or net profit). Net income results in an increase in owner's equity. A loss results in a decrease in owner's equity.

RETAINED EARNINGS: The amount of net income earned and retained by the corporation. If net income is like the score after a single basketball game, retained earnings is the lifetime statistic. Retained earnings is found in the equity section of the balance sheet. It keeps track of how much of the total owner's equity was earned and retained by the business versus how much capital has been invested from the owners (**paid-in capital**). It's what's left after everything's been paid - including taxes. It's the money the company can call its own.

Each month, the net profits are reflected in the balance sheet as current earnings. At the end of the year, current earnings are added to the retained earnings account.

Order Information

Use this convenient form to order products from MAXROHR Coaching Basic Business Skills.

Buy these helpful products — 100% NO PROBLEM Money Back Guarantee!

Name: _____

Address: _____

City / State / Zip: _____

Phone: _____

Fax: _____

	Price:	Quantity:	Order:
"How Much Should I Charge?" by Ellen Rohr	$19.99	_____	_____
"Where Did the Money Go?" by Ellen Rohr	$15.99	_____	_____
"Where Did the Money Go?" Audiotape	$19.99	_____	_____
Numbers Cruncher© Software	$249.95	_____	_____

Subtotal = $_____

Shipping
Orders $15.99 to $50 add $3.00 $_____
Orders over $50 add $6.00 $_____

Subtotal = $_____

MO residents add 5.1% sales tax $_____

TOTAL = $_____

Credit Card (VISA, MC and American Express accepted)

Card Number:_____ Exp. Date:_____

Order via mail, fax or telephone:
MAXROHR Coaching Basic Business Skills
3120 S. Know It All Lane
Rogersville, MO 65742
Toll-Free: 877-MAXROHR
Phone: (417) 753-3998
Fax: (417) 753-3685